D1091333

GOD, IMPROV, AND THE ART OF LIVING

God, Improv, and
the Art of Living

MaryAnn McKibben Dana

WILLIAM B. EERDMANS PUBLISHING COMPANY
GRAND RAPIDS, MICHIGAN

Wm. B. Eerdmans Publishing Co.
2140 Oak Industrial Drive NE, Grand Rapids, Michigan 49505
www.eerdmans.com

Published 2018
Printed in the United States of America

27 26 25 24 23 22 21 20 19 18   1 2 3 4 5 6 7 8 9 10

ISBN 978-0-8028-7464-1

Library of Congress Cataloging-in-Publication Data

Names: McKibben Dana, MaryAnn, author.
Title: God, improv, and the art of living / MaryAnn McKibben Dana.
Description: Grand Rapids : Eerdmans Publishing Co., 2018.
Identifiers: LCCN 2017059259 | ISBN 9780802874641
    (hardcover : alk. paper)
Subjects: LCSH: Christian life. | Improvisation (Acting)—Miscellanea. |
    Spontaneity (Philosophy)
Classification: LCC BV4509.5 .M3468 2018 | DDC 248—dc23
    LC record available at https://lccn.loc.gov/2017059259

For my children,
my best improv teachers

Contents

Foreword

When I was starting out as an actor, I had two passions: church and improv class. But I often felt like they were at odds with each other, because their approaches to life couldn't be more contradictory. Church taught me there was a plan for my life; my job was to decipher the plan and fulfill it. Improv taught me that there was no master plan or single truth. My job was to listen and discover whatever truth was unfolding onstage.

Of course I was a good Lutheran gal and went the church route. But I often left church filled with dread: *What if I miss the plan? What if I do it wrong?* I left improv class feeling invigorated: I'd participated in the act of creating something out of nothing. I didn't know how to reconcile the two ideas.

Years later my high-school sweetheart told me, "The biggest problem I had with you becoming a Christian is you lost all your spontaneity." I wanted to tell him I only accepted insults at 5 p.m. on Tuesdays. But I knew he was right. In my obsession to fulfill some plan, I'd become exhausted. I *had* lost my spontaneity—and my joy.

If only *God and Improv* had been written back then. I might have integrated the two passions in my life and saved myself the years of anguish.

MaryAnn McKibben Dana is an ordained pastor and a student of improvisation, so what's not to love? She's deftly brought the rules of improv and Christian spirituality together, and the result is a profound and engaging guidebook on the art of living. She even includes improv-based exercises to apply to one's spiritual life. Genius!

McKibben Dana invites us to approach life as a chance to discover with God, with all the mess and surprise that comes along with it. What if God isn't an immutable taskmaster but a creative collaborator? What if God's answer is "Yes And"? What if God is asking *us* the question: "What do *you* want?" It's a terrifying and freeing invitation. It's also a step toward maturity.

God, Improv, and the Art of Living doesn't shy away from difficult and insoluble dilemmas, either. If you've ever gotten an earful from Job's accusers, you know that platitudes and aphorisms will kill your soul. This book wades in deep and offers a better way through those Dark Nights of the Soul. We can learn to accept failure and ambiguity without capitulating to them. We can respond to tragedy and loss, as McKibben Dana puts it, by "fighting back with beauty."

I love this book. I'm making it the next book for my women's small group. And we're going to do improv!

Susan E. Isaacs

Introduction

It *plays among the arts.*
It's *indispensable in parenting.*
It *shows up in business, science, and sports.*
It *can help sharpen memory, stave off dementia,*
and combat writer's block.
It's improvisation, and according to Tina Fey's book *Bossypants*,
it will change your life and reduce belly fat.

Lamentably, the fine print assures us that improv does not
really reduce belly fat.[1] But the life-changing part is true.

*   *   *

Think for a moment about a time in your life when everything
went according to plan.

I'll wait for you to stop laughing.

Those moments seem rare, but I bet you can think of an
experience when things fell into place as you expected. A great
road trip. The perfect date. The career goal that came to pass.
Moments like these can be wonderful gifts of grace.

Now think about a time when the plan got completely
derailed—when life threw you a curveball—and how you

responded. The marriage proposal never came. The fertility treatments didn't work. The company downsized.

Chances are you had to rely on your wits and your community to get through it, making the best of the circumstances life handed you. Fumbling your way along, you surrendered to not knowing what was waiting for you around the bend. You improvised.

And you learned that your well-laid plans don't always rule the day. There can be gifts of grace in those unplanned experiences too. Sometimes.

We're all improvisers, often without realizing it. We improvise in order to get through the day. We improvise when life surprises us. We do it without even thinking about it.

This book will help you do it better.

✳   ✳   ✳

Chances are the word "improv" evokes certain images for you, not all of them positive. Most of us think immediately about comedy shows like *Whose Line Is It Anyway?*, and the thought of getting up onstage without a script might make you break out in virtual hives. You may wonder why you ever shelled out money for this book, or why your sadistic friend chose to give it to you.

I can relate.

As a high school and college student, I took part in a number of plays and musicals. I loved every moment of the process, but I remember the relief I felt when the rehearsals were over and I finally had the lines memorized. I knew what to say, what to do, and when to do it.

I come to this topic not because it comes naturally to me, but because it doesn't. Efficiency and organization are my twin superpowers. But live long enough and you realize that even the most bulletproof plans and expectations can get thwarted. Over time I found my way into this strange world of improv as a way of coping. Through meeting people who pursued improv as both an art form and a life practice, I began to wonder whether there was a better way to live than by clutching the plan ever more tightly. And now that I've discovered improv, I can't get enough of it. As Amy Poehler told *The New Yorker*, "We all think we're in control of our lives, and that the ground is solid beneath our feet, but we are so wrong. Improvising reminds you of that over and over again."[2]

Many of us are intrigued by improv but bring a set of misconceptions about it. Maybe we think it's about zaniness, being funny, or thinking quickly on our feet. Certainly a good improv show can contain all of those things, but those aren't the building blocks.

In my explorations with improv, I've had to unlearn a lot about myself, and what I thought it meant to do improv. Let me save you some time. Here's what improv is *not*:

Improv isn't about being clever or witty. As we'll see, the primary goal of improv isn't to be funny. The biggest payoff comes when two or more players create something authentic and real together. A scene. A project. A life.

Improv isn't spontaneous. There's an effortless quality to good improv, such that you can sometimes think it's plucked out of thin air. But behind each improv performance is a great deal of preparation—sometimes years. This book will help prepare you to do beautiful improv.

Improv isn't a free-for-all. Sometimes an improv show or scene can seem like a madcap bundle of manic energy. It's totally outside the box. But if you watch improv long enough, you see an underlying structure. There's an internal logic at work. We'll look more deeply at that structure together.

Improv isn't frivolous. Improv gets written off as a frivolous pursuit, something that's fun but light, a cotton-candy confection that lasts but a sweet moment on the tongue. But what could be less frivolous than learning how to navigate a complex world in which so much is out of our control?

So then, what *is* improv?

Improv is creative. Improv requires us to be light on our feet. It makes something happen. It creates. When we improvise together, literally anything can happen.

Improv is invigorating. Confession: as an introvert, I have to steel myself to get to improv class each week. It would take so much less effort to watch Netflix or putter around the house. But somehow, I scrape myself off the couch and get myself to class for two and a half hours of hard work. And I never, ever regret going. I leave energized and happy.

Improv is character-forming. As pastor Ashley Goff likes to say, "Improv is the most fun you'll ever have in therapy." I've learned more about myself in my study of improv than I have in almost any other endeavor. It's on-the-job life training.

Improv is risky. With improv, you never know what will happen. That's risky business. Several years ago, I led a workshop for a youth ministry event called "Sacred Movement," focused on praying with our bodies through drama and movement. When I arrived to set up the workshop, I found a sign on the classroom door: "***Scared*** Movement." There's always a bit of scared in the sacred. It's frightening to admit we're not in control, to chuck the ten-year plan and live more intuitively, more improvisationally. It's also a great adventure—strange and perplexing and wondrous.

Improv is play. When improvisers talk about what they do onstage, they almost never say, "I work with so-and-so in this group." Instead they say, "I play every Monday night," or "She and I play together." Extraordinary! Life is deadly serious sometimes. And sometimes it's *play* that creates a bridge to deeper understanding, self-awareness, and transformation. As G. K. Chesterton said, "Angels can fly because they can take themselves lightly."

*　　　　*　　　　*

Each section of this book explores a principle of improv and, by extension, an improvising life. Woven throughout are examples of how I've seen these principles lived out onstage, in the "real world," and in the Christian story. These seven principles aren't just coping mechanisms or tricks we use to get by. They are also ways of seeing God operating within God's world, in Scripture and in life, again and again. Although I write as a person of Christian faith and a pastor, I aim to offer insight to a wide range of readers. As I show how I see the world, I hope that these readers—actors, creatives, faith leaders, and others—will be helped in approaching the spiritual life with renewed vitality.

Because the lab of improv is on the stage, I'm going to be talking primarily about actors on a stage, playing a game, creating a scene, or performing a one-act play. While there's a lot to say about improv in other art forms—for example, riffing in jazz or freestyling in hip-hop—I'm not the person to write that book. But what little I know of these other genres suggests there's great overlap among them. And I suspect many of the same principles would apply.

Finally, I write this book from the perspective of a novice improviser. I've taken a bunch of classes in Washington, D.C., and at Second City in Chicago; I've taken part in showcases, performances, and jams; and I've shared these ideas on the road as a presenter at retreats, conferences, and workshops. But the more I learn, the more I realize how much I don't know. I appreciate veteran improvisers who've read excerpts of this book and talked through the topics with me. But I'm no expert. And as a self-described control freak with a perfectionistic streak a mile wide, I can't claim to have transformed my life into one of effortless ease and grace. What I *can* claim is that this book expresses my enthusiasm for a topic I'm only beginning to understand and embody.

My hope for you as a reader isn't necessarily that you become a fan of improvisational comedy. It's OK if you never sign up for an improv class. Heck, it's OK if you never attend a show as an audience member. What I want to do here is to share what improv has taught me and explore how lessons learned onstage translate to tools and practices that guide our emotional, social, vocational, and spiritual lives. And my hope is that you'll find those tools valuable.

In order to bring you a book that's exploratory and practical, I've also included exercises for each chapter at the end of the book—some for individuals and some for communities, families, and friends. And I do hope you'll try those. Don't be like the people in the old *New Yorker* cartoon who encounter two heavenly staircases ascending to the clouds. One staircase is marked "Heaven," while the other, much more popular staircase is marked "Discussion about Heaven." Do the work. And for our purposes, the work is to play.

Say Yes

There's a tiny word. It's not a noun, it's not a verb, it's not an adjective—I don't know what it is. But if you said it to me tonight, all this blackness would go away, and you and I would be connected by a tunnel of light.

—C. D. Bales, played by Steve Martin in the movie Roxanne[1]

The word, of course, is Yes.
And it's where all improvisation begins.

Chapter 1
Live Yes-ly

Many years ago, I worked with a church in Houston's Third Ward, an economically depressed area of town. The neighborhood embodied a paradox, so common in some urban neighborhoods, of dignity mingled with despair. Although the people I met were proud of their neighborhood's history and culture and worked to make it better, without significant opportunities for economic advancement, it was an uphill climb.

The local Episcopal church stood next to a liquor superstore—an example of the contradictions in the neighborhood. The door to the church office overlooked the side of the store, a bare wall that proved tempting for the young people in the area who frequently tagged it with graffiti.

Both the business and the church fretted over the defacement and had gotten into an arms race with the gangs. The wall was painted over numerous times. But the graffiti would return, the artists apparently grateful for the blank canvas. And on it went, world without end.

Finally the church decided to work with a local artist to design a mural for the wall. The storeowners, out of ideas, went along with it. The artist's task was to make sure the resulting design incorporated the spray-painted tags—not highlighting them, but not hiding them, either. Instead, they would be part of the overall image. After planning a design, the artist invited children from the church's day camp to help with the painting.

If you knew what you were looking for, you could see the original graffiti within the crazy-quilt of colors and patterns. According to folks at the church, the wall was a way to say, "We see you. We see the despair and the acting out. We aren't going to deny it. It's part of the story of the Third Ward. But we need to move past this conflict." The church realized that the graffiti was not a problem that could be easily solved. So instead, they reached out to embrace the community, even the parts of it that were destructive and tough to love.

The church said Yes.
The church improvised.

Any student or teacher of improv knows the first rule of improv: say Yes. Actually, the first rule is "Yes, And." But we'll get to "And" in Section 2 of the book. "And" is the 200-level course, and most of us need to start with the basics. We need to deal with Yes first, get it lodged in our hearts and minds and bodies, because we live in a world saturated with No. Too many voices in our culture speak the language of safety, scarcity, and fear. Over time these No messages end up adhering to us like sad, misshapen barnacles, weighing us down with what seems impossible, impractical, or simply ill-advised.

Incorporating graffiti into a mural may seem ill-advised. It's wrong to deface property. It sends the wrong message to let the vandalism remain there. Better to work with police to root out the culprits.

And yet the church staff told me with pride that once the mural appeared, the wall was never defaced with graffiti again. In fact, the mural project became a much-needed bridge to the young people in the community.

The church couldn't change what had happened. Instead, the people there accepted it as the place they needed to start—the reality as it was handed to them. They said Yes.

✻   ✻   ✻

Improv doesn't happen without Yes. In fact, *life* doesn't happen without Yes. Hopefully, each of us was nurtured by families and loved ones who said Yes to keeping us clothed and fed and loved. Teachers said Yes to teaching us to read so we could hold this book in our hands and comprehend it. However imperfectly they said that Yes, say it they did. Even those of us who had more than our share of No growing up had just enough Yes to bring us to today. Because we survived. We're still here.

As a Presbyterian pastor, I sit in a lot of church meetings. (The joke is that Presbyterians do things "decently and in order.") We have no bishops—the gathered community is the "bishop"—so we deliberate a lot. Many of these meetings end with a vote, usually a voice vote. And it's striking to hear how different Yes sounds from No. (Sometimes we use Aye or Nay when we're feeling fancy, but the phenomenon is the same.)

There is palpable energy when people say Yes. The word is crisp, sibilant. You can do a reluctant, lugubrious Yes if you try. But the essence of Yes has real power.

The word No can also carry a lot of force. Sometimes the No side prevails in these Presbyterian votes. But there's rarely much vigor to it. No doesn't get you out of bed in the morning. No doesn't offer a jolt of spiritual caffeine when your energy is flagging.

Try it now. Say Yes. Stand up and assume a Yes posture as you do it.

What position did your Yes take? I'm guessing your stance was solid and strong. Maybe your hands were curled into resolute fists. Or planted firmly on your hips. Or perhaps your arms were stretched wide open.

Now say No. What does a No posture look like? There's such a thing as a defiant No—we'll get to that in a later chapter—but most Noes aren't like that. No has arms folded across the chest. No has hunched shoulders. No is loath to look you in the eye.

Trust me, I know.

*   *   *

I'm drawn to improv not because I'm an effortless improviser, but because my default position is to resist Yes. I'm often tired or fearful of doing the new thing. I'm too worried about waste—wasted time, wasted effort. When I do muster up the gumption for a Yes, I can be reluctant or tentative, wondering what the neighbors might think. Or I say Yes with the posture of a martyr: *I'm agreeing to this, but I hope you can tell from my aggressive sighing that I'm not happy about it.*

As a writer and a work-from-home parent, I go to great lengths to set aside days just for writing: no meetings, no kid responsibilities. It has become almost comical, the ways those days can get hijacked, often by some petty illness that strikes one of my children without warning. So I find myself tiptoeing around in advance of my writing days, as if my plan is a bomb that will explode with one wrong step.

I scheduled one of these writing days recently, and that morning, I sat around the kitchen table as my unsuspecting children ate breakfast, hale and hearty, each one. *Could it be? An uninterrupted day?* I sent them out the door with my husband and prepared to settle in. Bliss.

Two minutes later Robert was back: his car battery was dead, and he was late for a meeting. Could he take the other car to work, and could I possibly handle it? *Oh, and after the roadside assistance guy comes later in the morning, you'll need to drive the car around for a while to get the battery charged up again.*

Yes. I could handle it and I did handle it. I won't lie—there was sighing. But I also realized that if this temporary interruption derailed my whole day, I had nobody but myself to blame.

When life's interruptions strike, there's not always a choice about whether to say Yes. It's not like I can will my child not to be sick, or bring the car sputtering instantly to life. In these situations, the Yes comes in *how* we react to the unexpected. An improvisational Yes holds our plans and expectations lightly: life happens, and we need to be flexible enough to adjust to its surprises—and even embrace them.

In the movie *Roxanne*, C. D. Bales wonders what kind of word Yes is. I had to look it up myself. "Yes" is actually an adverb. Most adverbs, you may recall, describe how something is done. I sing *loudly*. I drive *recklessly*.

So Yes isn't merely *what* we do when we improvise, but *how* we do it.

I can set aside my plans in order to care for a sick child *grudgingly*. I can meet the roadside assistance guy *resentfully*. Or I can do these things Yes-ly: with grace, and with the expectation that something surprising may occur. And even if the unexpected grace doesn't happen, it's still worthwhile to let my impeccable plans get disrupted. The lesson is the same for all of us. We are not in control of our lives. But we can choose Yes.

Chapter 2

Accept What We Can't Change

My father was a recovering alcoholic, and when I was growing up, our whole family attended twelve-step meetings. Alcoholics Anonymous for Dad, Al-Anon for Mom, Alateen for me, and Alatot for my younger siblings. My memories of these meetings are vague: a Methodist church overrun by people, many of whom smoked on the outdoor walkways and patios. Coffee urns and warm hugs. Long, unhurried stories. Tears and flashes of raw emotion that sometimes scared me. Rituals with recited slogans and clasped hands. And the Serenity Prayer:

> *God, grant me the serenity*
> *To accept the things I cannot change,*
> *The courage to change the things I can,*
> *And the wisdom to know the difference.*

I always assumed the prayer was original to AA, as I assumed many of its most beloved catchphrases were. How could it not be? It encapsulates so much of the personal and family dynamics of addiction. An alcoholic can't choose the way his or her body metabolizes booze. A spouse can't control an alcoholic's behavior or convince the person to stop drinking. A child of an alcoholic can't change the family system he or she inhabits. But there are things that each of us can change—namely, ourselves—and we need the wisdom to know what work is ours to do.

Once I went to seminary, I learned the Serenity Prayer began outside of twelve-step programs. There are many versions of the prayer and stories of how it came to be, but it's been most reliably attributed to Reinhold Niebuhr, a Protestant theologian of the early twentieth century.[1]

The prayer has a life beyond AA. It could also be called the improviser's prayer. When we accept the things we can't change, we are embodying Yes.

When we live in a spirit of Yes, it doesn't necessarily mean we like what's happening. It doesn't mean that we would have chosen a given circumstance for ourselves. I've done enough improv to have had a fellow improviser suggest something onstage that made me cringe, that gave me an internal "Ugh." But there's freedom in knowing that it's not my job to talk the person out of it; in fact, to do so would violate the cardinal rule of improv. My job is to do my best to live out the reality that my partner has spoken into being.

Improv instructor and mental health professional Lisa Kays calls this the orange sky problem. She says, "If character one says, 'The sky is orange,' the sky is orange. We cannot refute or argue this. However, that doesn't mean we have to like that the sky is orange. It can make our character sad, or confused, or scared. We can react to the sky being orange in any way, even with anger, but we can't dismiss the idea or argue with the premise itself. This is what agreement means in improv."[2]

TJ Jagodowski and Dave Pasquesi are two veteran performers who've been improvising a one-act play together every week for the past twenty years. They base this improvisation on ... nothing. No audience suggestion, no pre-set formula. They pluck the story out of the air. We'll talk more about TJ and Dave later. But one of their guiding principles is that while *characters* may disagree onstage, the *improvisers* must always agree. This means that the characters may experience conflict, but the players are grounded in the same reality. We don't have to see a partner's offer as a good thing, but an improvised life depends on acknowledging the offer honestly. That's the Yes that's required.[3]

*   *   *

Nancy Roman isn't a household name, but it should be. If you've ever been wowed by the image of a dying star with gases pluming out like butterfly wings, or of the haunting Pillars of Creation in the Eagle Nebula, you have her in part to thank. Nancy Roman oversaw the Hubble Space Telescope project for NASA for some two decades, and worked in the field of space exploration and research for even longer.

But NASA was never part of her plan. Instead, Roman began her career in academia, earning her Ph.D. in 1949, and prepared to settle into a life as a professor. But as a woman in a technical field in the 1950s, she couldn't find a university that would grant her tenure. After trying for a long time, she changed course. "In 1959," she says, "when NASA was formed, one of the men there asked whether I knew anyone who would like to set up a program in space astronomy. And I decided the idea of influencing space astronomy for fifty years was just more than I could resist, so I took the job."[4]

Nancy Roman didn't just set up the program. She was instrumental in getting Hubble developed, funded, and implemented, to the point that she's now known as the Mother of the Hubble. She accepted the thing she couldn't change, and changed the thing she could. She stopped hitting her head against the closed door, looked around, and found another way to serve. She found her Yes.

There's a strain of Christian theology that seeks to wrap up stories like Roman's with a tidy providential bow. "It was all meant to be," some might say. "Look what an impact she's had! Everything worked out for the best." Such theology strikes me as chintzy and cheap. Sexism is never "meant to be." And I have no doubt Nancy Roman would have had an impact wherever she went. What really happened here is that Roman had an orange sky moment. I don't know Roman's spiritual background, but I do know she embodies the spirit of Niebuhr's prayer. She accepted that she wasn't going to bust her way through the glass ceiling of a flawed university tenure system. Others could, and did, but instead she changed what she could—her own career path—and said Yes to an unexpected opportunity.

*　　　　*　　　　*

The universe offers untold possibilities to us. Yet I realize how much effort I've expended pounding on doors that remain resolutely locked. Sometimes, the work of accepting what we can't change involves letting go. It's not an easy process. As Anne Lamott has lamented, "Everything I've ever let go of has claw marks on it."[5]

But if we can pull it off, living the Serenity Prayer can make life a little more graceful. So many of our Noes are rooted in denial. Denial robs us of time and energy we don't have, and it can even deepen the messes we find ourselves in.

I'm a recreational runner, logging between fifteen and twenty-five miles a week depending on what kind of race I'm training for. Some time ago I started feeling something strange in my left leg, but I told myself it was the normal muscle soreness that comes from training hard. I continued to run on it until the pain became too loud to ignore. After a few doctors' appointments and an MRI, I was diagnosed with a stress fracture in my tibia. In an instant, my upcoming racing plans evaporated, including a bucket-list marathon, and I was prescribed twelve weeks of complete rest. Even walking needed to be minimized in the beginning. "Every step will set you back," the doctor warned, sympathetic but stern.

The cruel irony is that my first nagging aches were probably a shin splint, a relatively minor problem that can often be corrected with several days of rest, perhaps some new shoes, and a change in running form. Thanks to my refusal to accept what was happening, my shin splint bloomed into a full stress fracture, and I was out for three months. If I'd listened to my body—if I'd come to terms with the thing I couldn't change and changed what I could—I might have avoided the bigger injury altogether. Now, when people ask me what caused my injury, I say, "A bad case of denial."

Chapter 3

Listen for God's Yes

Does God ordain the various events in our lives? Does everything happen for a reason? Does God provide a gentle nudge, but leave the rest to us? We'll plumb these questions throughout the book. For now, let me argue that, whatever you think about God pulling strings or guiding life's events, improvisation is at the very center of how God interacts with us. Because, at the heart of it, the story of the Christian God is a story of Yes.

Jesus's ministry is full of Yes. In the Gospel of John, Jesus's very first sign is at a wedding in Cana, where he turns water into wine so the feast can continue. But he doesn't want to do it at first. His mother tells him, "They have no more wine," only to be rebuffed by her son: "Woman, what concern is that to you and to me? My hour has not yet come."

But then ... Jesus relents (John 2:1–11). We don't know whether he had something different in mind for his inaugural sign. But it seems possible. After all, his other signs in John are grand and bold. Walking on water. Feeding five thousand people. Raising a man from the dead.

Restocking the bar at a wedding? As first signs go, it's not a big Wow out of the gate. But Jesus's first sign in John's Gospel may be my favorite—because it's the one Jesus never planned to perform. It isn't on his agenda. The timing isn't right, he insists to his mother.

Yet the situation presents itself, and he says Yes. We aren't told exactly why. Perhaps it's for no other reason than to keep the party going late into the night. Or maybe he does it to please his mother. In any case, it's an act of simple beauty, not as grand, perhaps, as some of the other signs. Yet it reveals Jesus to be someone who will seek out the Yes.

It's an extravagant Yes because the gesture isn't necessary. It has little utility. It's just lovely, for love's sake.

∗   ∗   ∗

You'll meet the improvising Jesus again and again in this book. And it's one thing to see the heart of an improviser in Jesus. After all, Jesus is human, and humans improvise. But what about God? Christian theology teaches that Jesus is also fully divine. So why wouldn't God's nature also be improvisational?

We meet an improvising God constantly in Scripture. God experiments, changes God's mind, and works in partnership with God's people to bring about the Yes that's at the heart of improv—and also the gospel.

A mentor likes to remind her seminary classes that the book of Exodus—the story of God's liberation of the people of Israel from slavery into the Promised Land—has a clue about the nature of God right in the title. "Exodus" is a Greek word and literally means "a way out."[1] Not *the* way out, *a* way out. This subtle commentary says something of the infinite creativity of God. This doesn't sound like a God who planned how everything was going to turn out down to the last detail. This is a God who worked with the situation at hand. The "how" of God's work is incidental; the overarching Yes of liberation is God's fundamental focus.

In my religious tradition, we tend to describe God by using words like "immutable," "infallible," "certain," and "absolute." These words seem way too rigid to suggest an improvising God. But then there's the Holy Spirit, alive and at work in ways that seem to transcend such sturdy words. The Spirit is active, working and playing, through us and in spite of us, seen and unseen, making things new.

We see the Spirit at work in Exodus, providing a way out, moving the people away from the No of captivity to the Yes of freedom. I love the idea that God might have provided "a way out" in any of a hundred different ways, but instead God thought, *Hey, this will do: Moses ... Ever-escalating plagues ... Passage through the Red Sea ... Forty years of kvetching ... Let's do it.* That's a creative and fascinating deity. That's a God I want to know and follow—way more than a God who wrote down everything that was going to be, hit Save on Microsoft Word, and commenced the Big Bang.

*   *   *

An improvising God may also help us wrestle with questions of God's activity in the midst of suffering. When a tsunami sweeps through Asia, or horrific violence rampages through an elementary school, it's natural to wonder where God is in the midst of it all. These questions are ever-present. Job is the patron saint of these questions.

In the book of the Bible that bears Job's name, everything is taken away from him—his livelihood, his children, his health. Only his wife remains, who begs him to curse God so he can die. (Whether that's to put him out of his misery or hers is unclear.) He also has three friends who spend the rest of the story engaged in a grim post-mortem of Job's situation: *Come on, buddy. You must have done something to bring this on.* Job rejects their premise—and even if he did do something, Job retorts, the punishment is way out of proportion to whatever crime he may have committed against the Almighty.

As a pastor, I have walked with people during some of the most terrible circumstances imaginable. A few of them found comfort in the idea that their suffering was part of God's overall purpose and plan. But many more found no comfort in such notions. What kind of God would will terrible things to happen?

Instead, they were determined not to let their heartbreak be the last word. They believed—as I believe—that God was fiercely present in that suffering, moving them in the direction of wholeness and hope and Yes. They believed this because they felt the shift of Yes happen, sometimes over a long, wrenching period of time. They believed this because the God we meet in Scripture is the crucified One on the cross, who endured the most devastating No the powers of the day could dish out—and turned it to Yes three days later.

Chapter 4

Say No to Say Yes

When I was in seminary, we were taught about three basic kinds of sermons. The first is a Yes sermon. It focuses on God's steadfast love that endures forever, that affirms God as a God of possibility. God is much more free than we can imagine, more loving than we can comprehend, and more gracious than we can fathom.

The second kind of sermon is a Go sermon. It focuses on our response to God's Yes: our call to serve others, feed the hungry, and work for the reign of God on earth. Because Jesus's love was an active kind of love, we are called to love actively. Because God's grace is abundantly for us, we respond out of gratitude.

I've preached many Yes and Go sermons, and both are important. Yes without any Go means that we're like athletes training for a tournament that never comes (or an improv class with no performance!). We've got no skin in the game. On the flip side, all Go but no Yes can be exhausting. Without relying on God, how much can we really hope to accomplish?

But there's a third kind of sermon, the No sermon. These are more rare, but vitally important. A No sermon explores God's limits—not in terms of what God is able to do, but what God is able to abide—or not abide. Injustice. Violence. Cruelty.

The God of Scripture draws boundaries and establishes norms (and even rules) for God's people. God says No sometimes! In fact, No is indispensable to the gospel. We beam at Jesus's Beatitudes, while forgetting that in Luke's account they're quickly followed by an equal number of woes. For every "blessed are the poor" there's a "woe to the rich." "No" sermons are often the prophetic sermons. When a photo of a Syrian refugee pierces our hearts, or the warming of the planet becomes too urgent to ignore, we turn to the language of No.

∗   ∗   ∗

What role does No have in an improvised life, oriented toward Yes? Ask any parent of a toddler, and they'll tell you that No is a powerful word. No enforces limits. It's a cry of agency: *This is not OK with me.* I say No when I'm anxious or tired. Self-care is important, and if we have no Yes to give, it's healthy to say No and pull back for a while.

Yet there are times when No isn't just necessary, but the most faithful and creative response. Isn't refusing to get up from a lunch counter or boycotting the city busses a powerful act of resistance? The civil rights movement and other acts of protest have always been punctuated by moments of saying No. *No, we will not go to the back of the bus. No, we will not be second-class citizens anymore.*

There is a place for No, but it's a No that's fueled by a much stronger Yes—a thirst for justice, liberty, and freedom.

When I first started learning improv, I thought saying Yes meant going along with whatever my scene partner initiated. As

I said earlier, it's important to accept the premise of a scene—if a person points an improv gun at you, you can't say, "That's not a gun; that's a banana!"—but that doesn't mean you need to consent to be robbed. Conflict can be powerful creative fuel. It's a No—*I'm not handing you my wallet*—in service to a larger Yes: *What does the mugger do now? This scene could get interesting!* Saying No is empowering, especially for those of us who've been socialized to follow the rules and do what we're told.

Andrew Foster Connors is a pastor and community organizer in Baltimore. For decades there, members of the religious community and other organizations have come together to advocate and agitate for justice, racial reconciliation, and economic opportunity. Foster Connors is also a student of the civil rights movement, which influences the organizing work he does today. It's hard, incremental work.

I asked him how he understood the interplay of Yes and No, both in his work and within the struggle for civil rights. He told me,

> Well, we're all a part of power structures, and those power structures assume they have our consent when they act in certain ways. So a lot of what we do comes down to withdrawing our consent—bringing people together to say with one voice, "You can't proceed without our Yes, and we no longer give that to you." People in power are always shocked that people have the power to withdraw consent.

Foster Connors added that organizations do a lot of analysis and discernment to decide what kind of change to push for, and how quickly to do that. Sometimes the Yes seems out of reach, so the answer is No, or Not Yet. "Although sometimes for people of faith," he said, "it's important to voice opposition to injustice, even if you know you can't win." That, too, is part of withdrawing consent, of saying No. Even if we can't stop the powers that be, we can be forceful in our opposition to oppression and unchecked power.

This opposition is an improvising move—taking what life offers and responding faithfully to it. The No isn't an end in itself, but one of the tools we wield to forge a deeper Yes.

∗   ∗   ∗

In her Magnificat, Mary, the mother of Jesus, provides a template for this kind of No-wrapped-in-Yes. After becoming pregnant with Jesus under strange and miraculous circumstances, Mary is so moved by the power of God that she sings—not a gentle lullaby, but prophetic words:

> God has shown strength with his arm;
> God has scattered the proud in the thoughts of their
>   hearts.
> God has brought down the powerful from their thrones,
>   and lifted up the lowly;
> God has filled the hungry with good things, and sent the
>   rich away empty. (Luke 1: 51–53)

Mary's song is one of defiance, a defiance we will hear echoed centuries later in African-American spirituals and protest songs. It is "We Shall Overcome"; it is "Where Have All the Flowers Gone?" It is a dissent against the way things are, a counter-testimony to the dysfunction that passes for normal in our world.

Mary sings this song because her pregnancy itself is God's act of dissent against worldly power. God didn't choose a queen, a wealthy noblewoman to bear the Messiah. God chose an unmarried peasant girl. God assessed the demands of the world, and the expectations that a king would come in strength and might and prestige, and said, No, I'd just as soon not. And in her song Mary echoes this divine No. No to the proud and their haughty ways. No to hunger that goes unfed. No to suffering unrelieved. No, no, no.

Mary trusts that there's a larger, more brilliant, more interesting Yes still being revealed. It's the improviser's job to find that Yes—and sometimes No helps us to get there. Rather than stopping the action in its tracks, No fosters creative tension and provides the catalyst that keeps the action moving forward.

Chapter 5

Risk Yes

Jonathan Daniels was a well-to-do kid from rural New Hampshire who enrolled in Virginia Military Institute in the late 1950s. After his father died abruptly in his sophomore year, Jonathan's grief led to a reassessment of his priorities, and eventually he ended up in seminary. He was convicted by Martin Luther King Jr.'s call to come to Selma. There he witnessed the horrors his brothers and sisters were experiencing in Alabama. He would go back to Selma again and again—for a semester, for a summer—and in August 1965 he participated in a small protest and was jailed. After six days the group was released. While waiting for a ride home, they went into a grocery store to buy a drink. A deputy was threatening a black family, and Jonathan stepped in between them, pushing a young girl back out of the way. The deputy fired, and Jonathan was killed instantly.[1]

Jonathan Daniels said a Yes that cost him his life. He embodied preacher William Sloane Coffin's words about the kind of grace that allows us to "risk something big for something good."[2]

There's an assumption that improv is a happy-go-lucky, no-holds-barred art form. But that glosses over the reality that Yes is risky. Saying Yes onstage is risky. Saying Yes in the midst of one's life is even more so. And the risks don't always work out the way we want. If they did, life would be a series of sure things rather than a string of chancy improvisations.

In a commencement speech for Knox College, Stephen Colbert talks about the risks that come from saying yes:

> Now will saying "yes" get you in trouble at times? Will saying "yes" lead you to doing some foolish things? Yes it will. But don't be afraid to be a fool.... People who pretend to be wise to the ways of the world are mostly just cynics. Cynicism masquerades as wisdom, but it is the farthest thing from it. Because cynics don't learn anything. Because cynicism is a self-imposed blindness, a rejection of the world because we are afraid it will hurt us or disappoint us. Cynics always say no. But saying "yes" begins things. Saying "yes" is how things grow. Saying "yes" leads to knowledge.... So for as long as you have the strength to, say "yes."[3]

Yes is a hollow response if it doesn't come with the possibility of everything going catastrophically wrong. Yes is infused with curiosity, mystery, and a hint of danger. We don't know how life will turn out. It costs us something to step into that ambiguity.

*   *   *

My friend Sarah says the riskiest Yes she ever said was submitting an application to adopt a child. She had planned for it for years, and had completed all the paperwork. But when it was all done except for pressing the "Send" button, her finger hovered in suspended animation for a long time. Was she really ready for this? The potential heartbreak of getting matched with a child, falling in love from afar, and having the adoption fall through? And on the other side, the messy, heart-expanding, freedom-killing, tear-filled, joy-infused task of loving a child forever?

Click. Yes.

Some of us step into these Yes moments more easily than others. I myself prefer that my backup plans have backup plans. Many of us need to start small, with some less risky mini-Yeses to build a habit. Improv has been described as "creative cross-training," because it gives us tools and habits that translate to the rest of our lives.[4]

Many self-help books talk about creative risk in glowing terms. But sometimes our Yes crashes down, with hurtful impact. The gamble doesn't pay off, and hearts get broken. It's spiritually dishonest to suggest otherwise. As C. S. Lewis wrote, "Love anything and your heart will be wrung and possibly broken. If you want to make sure of keeping it intact you must give it to no one, not even an animal. Wrap it carefully 'round with hobbies and little luxuries; avoid all entanglements. . . . To love is to be vulnerable."[5]

*   *   *

Love itself is a risky Yes. When I was in training for ministry, I volunteered at Bo's Place of Houston, an organization that supported families who had lost a loved one—a parent or a child. I facilitated the teen group. After each meeting the volunteers would gather for debriefing. More than once, the counselor who worked with the parents would say with a heavy sigh, "These parents who've lost a child ... sometimes they just want to crawl into their child's casket with them." Grief was a physical presence they couldn't escape, a squatter in their house who refused to leave.

Saying Yes when life has pummeled us mercilessly takes an incredible amount of energy and stubbornness. Yet the parents I met in the grief program did just that. They got up every day, made the lunches, passed the photo of their lost one in the hallway, fell apart, got it together, and drove the carpool. They faced the pain again and fumbled their way toward the day's Yes, one improvisation at a time.

The Art Institute of Chicago has an exhibition of the photography of Gordon Parks paired with the prose of Ralph Ellison, the goal being to combine images and stories from Harlem. When I visited, one photo caught my eye: a client at the Lafargue Clinic, his head in his hands. The caption read, "The Lafargue Clinic aims to transfer despair, not into hope but into determination."[6] I was struck by the substitution— despair into *hope* is the common cliché. Yet sometimes hope is beyond our fumbling grasp; determination is the best we can do.

Learning to improvise means letting go of expectations— of success or positive outcomes or even progress. Our job is to respond to the offer. We don't know where the scene is going to go; saying the next Yes is what matters.

*   *   *

Long ago a therapist asked me, "What is it costing you to do nothing in this situation? And what would it cost you to act?"

We act when the costs of doing nothing are higher than the risks of stepping out and taking a chance—of having the difficult conversation or confronting an unhealthy relationship.

So Yes costs something. But No often costs more—it's just that the cost may be hidden. We get stuck, complacent. We settle for nothing special because it's easier, and seems to demand less of us.

The Quaker educator and writer Parker Palmer tells about a retreat he led some years ago with a group of government workers from Washington, D.C. Many of them got involved in public service out of a sincere desire to help people, but over the years they had become jaded and discouraged by a system in which the common good often takes a backseat to power and politics. One man was a former farmer who now worked for the Department of Agriculture. He told the other folks on the retreat that he had left behind on his desk an administrative action related to thinning topsoil in Midwestern farmland, which is a big environmental problem. The administrator in him knew what he was supposed to do, but he couldn't reconcile what was expected of him with what his farmer's heart knew was right. He felt stuck.

The last day of the retreat, the man told the group that he hadn't slept much the night before; he realized that he had to resolve the issue of the thinning topsoil in a way that honored his farmer's heart. After a time of reverent silence, one of the others asked how he was going to face the reaction of his boss, who had been pressuring him vigorously to do the expedient thing, which he knew in his heart was wrong. His Yes would be risky, with no clear road map and no guarantee of success.

"If I do not do this," he responded, "a piece of me will die. And that is much more grave than the prospect of losing my job." And then he said, "I realized that I don't report to my boss. I report to the land."[7]

Saying Yes has consequences. It comes at a cost. But improvisers are willing to embrace the risks, knowing that the outcome is never clear. They know that saying Yes is a risk worth taking.

Principle 2

Say And

A young pianist was playing a Chopin prelude in my master class. He understood it intellectually, but he was unable to convey the emotional energy that is the true language of music. Then I noticed something that proved to be the key: his body was firmly centered in the upright position. I blurted out, "The trouble is you're a two-buttock player!" I encouraged him to use his whole body to flow sideways, urging him to catch the wave of the music with the shape of his body, and suddenly the music took flight. A new distinction was born: the one-buttock player.

—Benjamin Zander, The Art of Possibility[1]

Yes is the beginning of improv, but it's not enough. After we've accepted the reality that's been offered to us, we build on that reality by saying And. We make our own unique contribution, so that our scenes—and our lives—can move forward, maybe even take flight.

It requires our entire self, buttocks and all.

Chapter 6

Live toward And

With Yes firmly in our hearts and on our lips, the next question in improv is "Now what?" Yes by itself doesn't create anything. It doesn't move the action forward. As improviser/instructor Liz Joynt Sandberg likes to tell her classes at Second City Training Center in Chicago, "Nobody wants to see you in neutral."

Sooner or later, someone has to And. We can't just receive what life offers us. We must build on it. We offer our contribution so the people around us have something to build on themselves. One step at a time—one And at a time—we move forward into the future together.

The first thing to say about And is that it's not automatic. It's a conscious move that we make. We have a choice about whether to And or not.

In his book *Improvisation: The Drama of Christian Ethics*, theologian Samuel Wells uses the rules of improv as a way of viewing God's work in the world and our response to that work. He says we have three options when circumstances come our way.

We can block the offer. We can refuse to receive what's being offered: we can resist, say no, and run the other way.

God's people take this option numerous times in Scripture. Think of Jonah, whom God calls to preach to the people of Nineveh: "Cry out against it; for their wickedness has come up before me" (Jonah 1:2). God wants to send a prophet to correct their sinful ways, but Jonah doesn't want the job. Instead, he books passage on a ship bound for Tarshish (alternate name: Anywhere-But-Nineveh).

He blocks God's call. Or ... he *tries* to. Many of us know the rest of the tale—a big fish swallows Jonah, giving him three foul-smelling, claustrophobic days to contemplate his choice. Once the fish regurgitates him onto the beach, God approaches again: *So ... about that transfer to Nineveh.* And this time, Jonah relents.

We can accept the offer. According to Wells, option two is to receive what's given—to pick it up and acknowledge it, but otherwise to do very little with it. This is the Yes without an And.

Consider Jesus's parable of the talents, in which a rich man entrusts a sum of money to each of three servants (Matt. 25:14–30). Two servants take the funds, invest them, and double their money; the third servant buries his talent in the ground. He accepts the offer and adds nothing to the transaction. It's a safe thing to do—his master won't make any money, but at least he won't lose any either. But the servant is chastised by his master and, by extension, Jesus. This is no way to grow the reign of God, Jesus says: "To all those who have, more will be given, and they will have an abundance; but from those who have nothing, even what they have will be taken away" (Matt. 25:29). The way of Jesus requires more of our talents than a safe, secure burial in the ground.

Which leads us to Wells's third alternative:

We can "over-accept." This is how Wells describes the experience of Yes-And, of accepting the offer and building on it. This is the move of the improviser.[1]

In the biblical story there are many Yes-Ands. The most crucial is the hinge-point of Scripture for Christians: the life, death, and resurrection of Jesus. Jesus's message and his movement toward the reign of God lead directly to his execution by the powerful elite. But Jesus doesn't try to block this outcome—mounting an army to fight the forces of Rome, say, or stealing away to another country to live the rest of his days in seclusion. Nor does he merely accept the circumstances—submitting to death, remaining safely buried in the tomb, and letting that quietly be the end of it.

Instead, Jesus over-accepts, proclaiming forgiveness and grace for his executioners while hanging from the very cross that was meant to humiliate and defeat him. And the resurrection story is the ultimate Yes-And, a triumph over the grave. Jesus overcomes the crucifixion, putting the powers of death definitively in their place.

A call to convert Nineveh. A sum of money. An angry mob, bent on crucifixion and bolstered by an oppressive state. Wells, improbably, calls these situations "gifts." This is a term that's often used in improv workshops too: we give each other gifts onstage whenever we make an offer by uttering a line or establish a clear emotion in our characters. It gives our partner something to work with. But the word "gift" gets way more problematic once we move offstage and into the realm of real life. Not all gifts are welcome ones. (Ask any cat owner about the "gifts" their feline hunter leaves on the back doorstep.) Life frequently offers us circumstances that aren't even close to what we would put on our wish lists.

Wells uses the word "gift" literally and neutrally: a gift is simply a thing that is given. It's too chipper to suggest that every gift contains something *positive*. But gifts do often contain *potential*. We uncover that potential by saying And, then seeing what happens.

*   *   *

I appreciate Wells's description of the three alternatives but quibble with the term "over-acceptance." It doesn't encapsulate a process that can be wildly open-ended. Over the years I've worked with groups on improv and the spiritual life. Within these groups additional and complementary terms have emerged, uncovering different aspects of what it means to say Yes-And, to over-accept. The term that holds up most robustly is "embracing." No, it's not a perfect term. In embracing we can close our arms around ourselves, when what we want to do is find a way to open our arms wide and let the gift make us and others more free.

Still, this word resonates because in embracing, we're accepting our reality, not grudgingly, but committing our whole selves to what happens next. In the parable of the prodigal son, we can imagine the embrace of the father when his son returns home from his wayward wanderings. The embrace holds no recriminations. Instead, the father is joyful, grateful, pulling his son close to himself as if never to let go. Many situations call for just such a posture.

"We *had* to celebrate," the father tells his grumbling older son as he sulks outside the party. "What was lost has been found." But the celebration isn't a foregone conclusion—the father didn't *have* to celebrate; he *chose* to. My sense of justice puts me in sympathy with the older son, who did what he was told and wants his younger sibling to suffer for his recalcitrance. But I know which character embraced his wayward son, who improvised his way to radical grace. I know which character I'd rather be—and which character I hope God is.

Chapter 7

Listen for God's And

Earlier we considered Yes as the foundation of the biblical story. God is a God who says Yes. That Yes isn't static—it moves us somewhere. God always stirs us in the direction of more surprising grace, more radical community, and deeper wholeness. Which means the Bible is also a story of And.

Scripture contains stories of people in an ongoing state of improvisation—making do with meager provisions, building on situations, and surviving on their wits—all in relationship with a God who improvises right back. When faced with a world that they wouldn't necessarily have chosen for themselves, "And" is the people's affirmation of faith in the God who told Abraham that he and his barren wife would parent a great nation, and who told imperfect Peter that he would be the foundation of a great church. "And" is a tool for a scrappy God and God's resourceful people.

With thousands of years of religious tradition and cultural establishment firmly under our feet, and with a couple billion adherents around the world, Christians can easily forget that the Bible is the story of scoundrels and saints, of underdogs and scaredy-cats.

*   *   *

When the Pharaoh of Egypt begins to worry that the Hebrew people are becoming too numerous and may rise up
against him, he instructs the midwives attending the Hebrew
women's births to put the infant boys to death. It's a devastating instruction—slow-motion genocide.

What can insignificant midwives do against such power?
They find a small way to resist: they let the boys live, and
convince Pharaoh that the women are so hardy that they give
birth before the midwives are able to show up.

One of those infant boys is Moses. Placed in a basket
smeared with pitch among the reeds of the river, Moses is set
afloat by his family, and Pharaoh's own daughter finds him.
Moved by the sight of the infant, she says, "This must be one
of the Hebrews' children." Moses's sister sees her opportunity, emerges from her hiding place, and suggests a nurse for
the baby—Moses's own mother. So Moses grows up in the
royal palace, and in the fullness of time, anointed by God and
backed by the power of ten plagues, he demands the release of
the Hebrew people from slavery (Exod. 2–3).

And it all begins with a couple of midwives, a watertight
basket—and improv. Was the plan formed as a last-ditch, "we
have no idea what will happen" effort when all other options
were exhausted? Whatever inspired Moses's family to nestle
him among the reeds, it was just enough of an And to keep the
story going.

Throughout the Bible, improvisation is a tool of the pow-
erless against the powerful. Joseph, interpreter of dreams, improvises his way from prison dungeon to Pharaoh's house, in
perfect position to save his tribe when famine hits (Gen. 47).

Tamar improvises a bit of trickery against her father-in-law
to ensure she will have an heir, and thus a future (Gen. 38).
Naomi conspires with her daughter-in-law Ruth to endear
Ruth to Boaz so they will have security—and, as it happens, a
great-grandson, David, who will be crowned a king (Ruth 3–4).
Improv plays among a people thrust into exile who continue
to tell the stories and pray the laments and keep hope alive.
Because their God is an improvising God, who always has
another And up the divine sleeve.

*   *   *

Improv lives in the heart of Jesus, lord of the dance, whose
And is immortalized in the hymn that proclaims, "You cut
me down, and I leap up high; I am the life that will never,
never die."[1]

Jesus is a master of improvisation. He's constantly changing the conversation, defying easy answers, and confounding
religious authorities with his absolute refusal to be cate-
gorized and pegged. Martin Copenhaver writes that in the
Gospels, Jesus is asked 183 questions, and he himself asks 307
questions. How many questions does he answer? Three.[2]

I haven't checked the math, but it sounds about right.

*   *   *

Probably my favorite story of Jesus experiencing And is in
his exchange with a Syro-Phoenician woman (Matt. 15:21–28).
The woman comes to Jesus and asks him to heal her daughter,
but she's not a member of the tribe of Israel—she's an out-
sider. At first, Jesus tries Sam Wells's blocking move. When

she starts to call to him, he doesn't respond. He pretends he doesn't hear her.

When that doesn't work—because even the Son of God can only block for so long—she asks again for healing for her daughter. Then Jesus tries to rebuff her: "It is not fair to take the children's food and throw it to the dogs." It's an acceptance of a sort: *Yeah, I have the power to do that—just not for you, foreigner.*

What's going on? Is this Jesus's human side poking through the divine exoskeleton? Is Jesus toying with her to see what she'll do? I doubt I'll ever find a satisfactory explanation. All things being equal, I prefer a messiah that *doesn't* call women dogs.

But whatever was going on in Jesus's head, what happens next is the jewel of improv. The woman doesn't argue with him: *I am not a dog!* But neither does she slink off in despair and shame (as I probably would). Instead, she over-accepts. She embraces his metaphor and builds on it to make her point. "Yes, Lord, yet even the dogs eat the crumbs that fall from their masters' table."

Zing! This is improvisation at its best. She moves the scene forward—she moves *Jesus* forward. She says, *This kingdom you're proclaiming? It isn't about what's "fair." It's never been about what's fair. You, Jesus, are so much better than fair.*

And her over-acceptance inspires Jesus, too, to over-accept: "Woman, great is your faith! Let it be done for you as you wish." And her daughter is healed.

$$* \qquad * \qquad *$$

For those of us who want—who need—God to be steadfast and in control, such an exchange is perplexing. Is God really subject to such whims when it comes to the suffering of a young girl? What kind of God is this? And yet Scripture offers numerous examples of God changing God's mind. The first comes in Genesis, when God is ready to destroy Sodom and Gomorrah. God goes to Abraham and says, *I've had it with these people. Step aside.*

We see the divine temper next in the wilderness, when the tribes of Israel get anxious because Moses has been on the mountain with God too long, and they construct a golden calf to worship instead. God is *this close* to consuming them as a result. Imagine. God is ready to destroy God's chosen people, the people God loved and cherished so much that God led them out of Israel, caused the Red Sea to split in two to provide safe passage, and blanketed the desert with manna, just enough for everyone. I'm not saying the Israelites are blameless—not even forty days go by without word from Moses, and they're melting down their jewelry to make other gods to worship. And because God has come this far with them, God's anger is now so great that it threatens their very existence.

How does God turn things around? What happens to change things?

Abraham happens.

Moses happens.

Abraham says, *What if you could find fifty righteous people in Sodom and Gomorrah? Would you withhold punishment on the cities?* And God says yes. So Abraham presses on: *What about forty-five people? Forty? Thirty? Ten?*

And ten is the magic number. Because of ten righteous ones, God spares a whole community[3] (Gen. 18:16–33).

In the wilderness, Moses doesn't need ten people—just three. After making various arguments to try to calm God's wrath against the calf-worshiping miscreants, Moses stumbles upon the formula:

Remember Abraham.
Remember Isaac.
Remember Jacob.
Remember the promises you made.

It is enough to remember those names. And God changes God's mind (Exod. 32:14).

*   *   *

Beautiful in their own ways, these stories are also disturbing. I'm unsettled by a God who changes course based on human intervention. Is God somehow beholden to us? This tension is also part of improv, something we'll deal with more fully later on. For now, it's enough to say this: Rather than being remote and impersonal, God's nature is to collaborate—to improvise— with God's people. And when that improvisation occurs, it moves in the direction of inclusion and mercy and grace.

The people of Sodom and Gomorrah are saved.
The people of Israel are spared.
The daughter of a foreign woman is healed,
and Jesus's ministry expanded.

Such is the power of the biblical And.

Chapter 8

Use And to Create Possibilities

What happens in our brains when we improvise? Several years ago, researcher and surgeon Charles Limb undertook a study to answer that question. Focusing his work on musicians, he rigged up a contraption that would allow them to play on a piano keyboard while reclining in an MRI machine. The musicians were asked to play simple scales, then spend time improvising on them. Not surprisingly, the parts of the brain that govern self-expression and creativity lit up during the improvisations. But more surprising is that other areas of the brain went quiet—specifically, the portions of the brain that govern inhibition.

Limb began asking other artists to be monitored in the machine—rappers, for example—and found a similar result. In order to be creative, he theorized, we need to subdue the parts of ourselves that govern self-consciousness and self-monitoring. "One area turns on, and a big area shuts off," Limb says, "so that you're not inhibited, so that you're willing to make mistakes, so that you're not constantly shutting down all of these new generative impulses." In other words, the process of saying Yes-And flows best when we're focused solely on that task rather than our own sense of propriety.[1]

For better or worse, we normally think of drugs and alcohol as the classic means for escaping inhibition. Plenty of artists and musicians lean heavily on these substances. But there are other ways of quieting the inner governor. This is one of the promises of improv, and why many people are drawn to it.

One of the things that makes Jesus so attractive as a personality is his lack of self-consciousness or inhibition. He remains always present, ready to Yes-And, and unconcerned about how something will "play." We, on the other hand, can be hounded by insecurity. *What will others think?* We avoid potential mistakes at all costs. But such anxiety inhibits our creativity and kills the spirit of And.

But that anxiety over "getting it right" is tough to quiet— and it seems to have been with us from the beginning. Maybe that's what the story of the Garden of Eden is about. When Adam and Eve eat from the tree of the knowledge of good and evil, that full knowledge includes awareness of their limitations and finitude. They cover themselves with hastily assembled garments of fig leaves because they're ashamed, inhibited.

What are the "fig leaves" we use to hide ourselves? Respectability. Prudence. Predictability. Routine. The inhibiting part of the brain is appeased, but the creative part is starved.

∗   ∗   ∗

One of the ways we choke off creativity is by suppressing And in favor of But. "But" is the favorite word of our sensible, inhibited selves.

But … it will *never work*.
But … it's *too expensive*.
But … I *just don't want to*.

In improv classes there are games that bring this dynamic to light. People get into pairs, and one person in each is assigned the task of convincing the other person to do something. ("Let's go on a tour of all the frozen yogurt places in the city!") Person #2's only job is to say No to every suggestion.

In the second round, every Person #2 can say, "Yes, but …" They're allowed to agree, but they must voice an objection. The third round is Yes, And. It's always apparent by the noise level that this generates the most energy and enthusiasm. But groups are often surprised to learn that "Yes, but …" is almost as deflating as a flat-out "No." *How can that be?* they wonder. *We're saying Yes!* The problem is that, even when coupled with Yes, "But" becomes a brake pedal, a dam we build to inhibit the flow of ideas.

I was once in a scene in which my scene partner had run over my pet turkey—I claimed it was her fault, but she put the fault back on me for letting the turkey out of the yard. I countered that I should be able to let my turkey roam free, the way nature intended, but she shot back. This went on for a few more lines until our instructor said, "Somebody lose the argument." One of us relented (I can't remember who), and the scene started moving forward again. We'd been stuck in an endless loop of "Buts."

Michael Auzenne and Mark Horstman, who work with business clients through their Manager Tools consulting firm and podcast, suggest a standing rule for meetings: to use the word "and" instead of "but." Nothing kills the spirit of collaboration faster than "but," they argue. Life offers us very few true absolutes, and two things that seem contradictory can both be true. The world is too complex to argue otherwise. "But" lacks nuance and closes discussion. "And" keeps things open.[2]

That's a great idea . . . and it's going to cost more. (Implied question: Are there places to trim costs so we could implement this idea? Is it worth it?)

We can try to ship the product earlier . . . and our team is going to have to put in longer hours to make it happen. (Implied questions: Is this a cost we're willing to bear? What would need to change and shift?)

Here's the thing about "and" and "but"—they're both promiscuous. They multiply. Only one of them, however, moves things forward. "But" dares the other person to dig in and counter with another "but." "And" gives space for ideas to grow.

The Manager Tools guys aren't saying that there are no absolutes in life. Sometimes two realities won't square with each other. Their point is that our language can flag when we're acting with a zero-sum mentality—when we're setting up barriers where there shouldn't be any.

*   *   *

Perhaps you saw the heartbreaking photo several years ago— an Episcopal church that was vandalized with a blunt, wrenching question spray-painted on an outside wall:

Will I still get to heaven if I kill myself?

The church could have blocked the situation—painted over the graffiti and never spoken of it again. Or they could have accepted—supported the local crisis hotline, or presented a sermon series on tough questions of faith. Perhaps they did those things. But they also embraced. They picked up a can of paint and wrote their own message: *God loves you with no exceptions.*

I can imagine all kinds of "But" statements from members of the congregation:

But vandalism is wrong.
But we can't condone this behavior.
But my children were baptized in this church.
It hurts to see it defaced in this way.

All valid perspectives. And yet. And yet. Photos of the church's response went viral, and the message of God's expansive love went way beyond their immediate community. All because they were open to a spirit of creative possibility. They were willing to improvise a greater And.[3]

Chapter 9

Embrace the Vulnerability of And

Keith Snyder is a writer, musician, and music nerd who still mourns the day that synthesizers became digital devices instead of analog ones. Apparently, when most digital synthesizers break, they simply stop working. No more sound comes out of them. But according to Keith, "When something goes wrong with an analog synth, you might get a really interesting sound, often musical in some way, which you could never get by moving the knobs and sliders on the synth the way they were designed to be moved." He still remembers plugging in an old Juno-6 after it had spent ten years in storage. Out came one of these happy accidents. "There was this awesome, never-to-be-heard-again burble, but now the circuits are all working to spec again, so there's no way to reproduce it," he laments.

Digital synthesizers break. But analog synthesizers break in interesting ways. Keith has turned this idea into a prayer:

May I break in interesting ways.

I'm intrigued by this prayer as guidance for improvisers. It takes courage to step into the unknown without a guarantee of success, a plan, or even a net. It will change us, touch our vulnerability, reveal our brokenness. The key for the improviser, then, is to see the brokenness not as a threat or a cause for shame, but as a source of strength. When we're willing to be broken in interesting ways, we allow ourselves to be part of a larger, unpredictable story.

*   *   *

A few years back, Princeton University professor Johannes Haushofer made a splash for posting what he called his "CV of Failures": degree programs for which he was rejected, fellowships he applied for and didn't receive, papers he submitted that weren't published—one closed door after another. And the biggest failure of all? He cheekily wrote, "This darn CV of Failures has received way more attention than my entire body of academic work."[1]

While I wish Professor Haushofer well in that academic work, I understand why his Failure CV captivated others. Most of us keep our failures private and our successes public. Which means we only see one another's Yes-Ands that bear fruit. This is a shame. Because not every "And" is a success. And yet we're still called to pursue them.

"[Hope is] something you put into practice," says radio talk-show host Krista Tippett. "We're learning through neuroscience [that] what you practice you become. And that goes for being more patient, being more hopeful, being more compassionate, just like it goes for any other skill." She continues,

> And so I think you can be—you can choose to be hopeful, which is a ... far more courageous choice than cynicism. I mean, cynicism is really easy. It's never surprised or disappointed. And doesn't lift a finger to change anything. [By

practicing hope], we can develop spiritual muscle memory. The more we do it ... it can become instinctive.[2]

To be committed to "And" is to be committed to a work that is grounded in hope. But this work doesn't come easily. And we may get our hearts broken in the process.

*   *   *

Several years ago, I was asked to apply for a major, high-profile position within the Presbyterian Church. I attacked that opportunity with everything I had. I talked to previous holders of the position. I spoke to people close to the organization. I assembled my posse of supporters and wise friends to help me think through how to put my best self forward. When asked to submit some representative work, I didn't play it safe—I took a risk and shared something that had a little edge to it. I shared ideas for how to help the organization survive and thrive. I interviewed for the job with everything I knew how to bring.

I left a MaryAnn-shaped hole in the wall.

And I was absolutely sure the position was mine right up to the precise moment the search committee chair told me they'd selected someone else.

In retrospect, there were signs I could and should have seen. A shift in mood among the committee between the phone interview and the in-person conversation. Some cautionary words from a friend of mine close to the search process. But it didn't matter. I had failed at something I'd really tried hard at. I'd brought a lot of people into the process, which made the failure public. And now I'm writing about it again, which means I'm reliving every cringe-inducing moment.

Should I have changed the way I approached this opportunity? When a similar opportunity arises in the future, will I be more careful, more guarded?

I don't know.
But I hope not.

*   *   *

When we improvise, we take a risk, not knowing where Yes-And will take us. In that sense, improv provides a different spin than the traditional "taking a leap of faith." As TJ and Dave write in their book, "Faith is not jumping from point A to point B. Faith is jumping from point A."[3]

Astronaut Mike Massimino was one of those charged with giving the Hubble Space Telescope some final tweaks in 2009. Unfortunately, a handrail got in the way of some of the team's repairs, and they came to realize they'd have to pry it off. There was no way to take it off piece by piece or bolt by bolt—it was going to come down to one big yank. Add in the capriciousness of zero gravity and not knowing whether shards would fly into other sensitive parts of the Hubble, and the risks were great. NASA teams on the ground did as many simulations as they could, and the astronauts on the shuttle did what they could to minimize the shrapnel, but ultimately … they had to let it rip.[4]

If it hadn't worked, Mike Massimino would have gone down in NASA history as the guy who broke Hubble. But it did work, so now he's known as the person who broke it in order to fix it. A parable, perhaps, for the kind of vulnerability we're talking about, which becomes essential to an improvised life.

Train Your Vision

To see what is in front of one's nose is a constant struggle.

—George Orwell[1]

Ask a random person the most indispensable quality in a good improviser, and they're likely to say, "They're quick. Clever. Funny."

Not really.

The most indispensable quality in a good improviser is the ability to listen and observe
… to see what others are doing onstage;
… to hear the emotion behind the words;
… to discern the authentic response within one's self to what's happening.

After all, if improv is built on a process of Yes-And, how can we say yes to the offer if we aren't listening for it? And how can we build in a spirit of And without absorbing what's been said?

Chapter 10

Cultivate Vision

Think about the best conversationalists at a dinner party, the ones you really enjoy talking to. Maybe you know one of those rare individuals who can spin a good yarn, or command the room like a charismatic leader. But more likely, that great conversationalist you're thinking of is probably a great listener—someone who asks good questions, who hears what others are saying, and who takes an active interest in others' perspectives.

Experienced improvisers will tell you that the true MVPs onstage are the good listeners. Deep listening is a gift. But it's also a skill that can be honed—both onstage and over the course of an improvised life.

I remember playing a scene in an intro class with Eric, a guy I really enjoyed improvising with. A laid-back type, he punctuated many of his scenes with "dude," regardless of the gender of his scene partner. But, like me, he wasn't instantly funny, so sometimes I'd feel a stab of anxiety when I got paired with him. (This was back when I thought the objective was to be funny. I later learned that "funny" is the by-product of authenticity and relationship, but as a novice, I didn't trust that yet.) I remember one of our pairings in particular.

I initiated: "We need to do something about Mom."

He responded quietly with a grimace. "Yeah, she's been so sick lately."

I shot back, "She keeps thinking the cat is a unicorn."

At this point our teacher stopped us—something he didn't often do, especially so early in a scene. "MaryAnn, that was a No you just gave Eric. He gave you an offering—'she's really sick'—and instead of building on it, you went in a totally different direction."

Guilty as charged. Not only did I fail to Yes-And Eric's offer; I'm not even sure I heard it. I had already decided what was wrong with Mom—*She's losing her marbles! Oh, how zany of me!*—and just waited for a moment to spring it on him. A total non-listening moment.

As improv instructor Julie Brister says, "When you're waiting for somebody to stop talking, what you're really doing is saying that you want to control the situation. Control is not a good thing in improv at all; it's not about trying to control what's going on. So eventually [in improv instruction] you get people to let go, and to really listen and be in the moment. But that can take some time and some work."[1]

That kind of work is relationship work. Therapists teach active listening to clients, in which one person repeats what's been said by the other to make sure they heard and understood. I did a variation of this exercise as a student at Second City. In pairs, person A makes a statement, and person B says, "You say ..." and repeats the statement word-for-word. Then they add to it: "And I say ..." Then it goes back to the first person, who must mirror and add:

Person A: It's been such a hot summer.

Person B: You say it's been such a hot summer, and I say, "I'm so glad we're on this plane bound for the North Pole."

Person A: You say you're glad we're on a plane bound for the North Pole. And I say, "I hope Santa likes the slippers we got him."

It's a clunky scene, and nothing you'd ever want to see onstage. But it keeps people from fake-listening to each other. You have to repeat what your partner said, then add something that organically flows from it, so it becomes very obvious when you're just going through the motions.

We simply can't improvise without paying attention—without seeing the person in front of us and hearing what's actually being communicated. It's one of the greatest ways of honoring another human being. There's nothing better than having someone acknowledge and embrace an idea we offered onstage (or in life). We feel heard, seen, and valued.

This kind of vision requires the practice of mindfulness and attention. It seems strange to connect mindfulness with improv—if we've seen rapid-fire comedy onstage, it doesn't seem to have much in common with a slow, deep practice of attentiveness so often relegated to religion and spirituality. Yet they're surprisingly linked.

It's hard to overstate how countercultural good listening is. We live in a sound-bite culture, punctuated with bulleted lists, talking points, and hot takes. Sherry Turkle, a professor of social studies of science and technology at MIT, studies how the constant flow of digital communication impacts conversation. And she's finding that people are losing patience for conversation. It's inefficient, with pointless detours and meanderings. It's not a "good use of time." And set aside face-to-face conversations; even *phone* conversations are diminishing in favor of texts and instant messages.[2]

But conversation, with its back-and-forth unpredictability, is the simplest form of improv, and as we move more interactions online, we're losing valuable skills. Getting the gist is now our default practice, to the exclusion of deep understanding and shared wisdom.

We sacrifice so much to sound-bite communication. Mystery. Subtlety. Even basic surprise. If contemplation is a "long, loving look at the real," as Jesuit theologian Walter Burkhardt has suggested, we are quickly settling for a short, judgmental glance off the surface.[3]

True listening trusts there is enough time to consider, absorb, and be changed. Onstage, a good improviser trusts that a little bit of awkward silence isn't nearly as bad as making a hasty move that doesn't honor what their partner has offered.

*   *   *

In an improv workshop a few years ago, my group was put into pairs and asked to stand face to face. For thirty seconds, we were to simply look at each other without speaking. At the end of that time, one person of the pair would make an offer, a single sentence or so. And the other would respond to it.

Did I mention the silence was thirty seconds long?

It was painful.

Some might have seen the game as an exercise in patience: to realize that the world won't come to an end if we don't act immediately, that it's OK to take a beat. I, instead, flew into an interior panic: *I'm looking at them, but they're looking at me too.*

I wonder what they're seeing? My eyes, bloodshot because I didn't get enough sleep last night? The mole on the side of my face? My gray hair?

If you're noticing that my anxiety over being seen got in the way of seeing my partner, you're quicker on the draw than I was.

This is one of the things I love about improv, though: there's nowhere to hide in an exercise like that. Improv is one of the most honest spaces I know, because what merely functions as subtext in so many other spaces can be brought into the open. I've always had a vague sense of walking around with a snarky interior voice of self-judgment narrating my actions. But it took just thirty seconds of silence to bring that voice screaming to the surface.

Why did I assume that the other person was looking at me critically? I wasn't looking at her that way. I'm guessing pretty much everyone is uncomfortable in an exercise like that, because everyone is vulnerable—but not always for the same reason. My partner may not be hearing commentary from Judgey McSnarksalot in her head, but there's something else going on inside of her, something equally strange and ultimately fruitful if she's willing to engage with it.

So, in thirty seconds I received a vision of myself and the self-critical voice I live with. What I would do next—how I would Yes-And that realization—is what improvising life is all about.

✳   ✳   ✳

One of my favorite improv games as both a participant and a leader is called "What Else Could This Be?" The premise is simple: you pass around an object—a pool noodle, an egg-beater—and ask people to imagine and pantomime other uses for it. (The pool noodle can be a set of horns; the eggbeater, a unicycle for a leprechaun.)

This game is a marriage of vision and imagination. The goal is to see the item in all its intricacies in order to imagine other uses for it. A church I once served as pastor underwent this re-envisioning exercise with a neglected sanctuary balcony. It was filled with dusty old books and ramshackle furniture—it had become a dumping ground for unused items nobody knew what to do with. After some rounds of "What else could this be?", we cleaned it out and transformed it into a worship space for children, complete with comfortable chairs, crafts, and picture books. Kids could hear the service (and frequently asked their parents questions on the way home from church about what they'd experienced), yet were given the freedom to move around a little more than they could on the hard pews downstairs.

James H. Crocker was a NASA engineer tasked with helping fix a defective mirror in the Hubble Space Telescope back in 1993. The mirror was deep in the telescope and not easily accessible for repairs—not to mention the fact that it had already been put into orbit 300 miles above earth, which complicated things. Crocker met with a team in Germany to discuss all kinds of scenarios and solutions, but the group was feeling stuck.

After a long, discouraging day of brainstorming, Crocker went back to the hotel to take a shower—and noticed that the showerhead was mounted on a bar that allowed it to be adjusted to any height.

What else could this be?

A solution to the defective Hubble? Crocker wondered what it would be like to put the corrective mirrors on robotic poles that could extend into the telescope, place the mirrors with accuracy down to millionths of an inch, and retract again.[4]

James Crocker had the vision to see what was right in front of him—and not only that, but to see the possibilities within it, to imagine a solution to help create a new reality.

It was a moment of improvised inspiration.

Chapter 11

Pay Attention

One of my pet interests is technology and the impact of digital communication on our emotional and spiritual lives. How do online interactions and social media change the way we relate to one another? How do they impact our sense of ourselves and the world?

A few years ago I put together a survey in which I asked people to think about their time spent online and what effect they felt it had on their mental and emotional wellness. More than a third of respondents said the Internet had negatively impacted their attention spans.

Nicholas Carr was one of the first to get this conversation going in his 2008 *Atlantic* article "Is Google Making Us Stupid?":

> Over the past few years I've had an uncomfortable sense that someone, or something, has been tinkering with my brain, remapping the neural circuitry, reprogramming the memory. My mind isn't going—so far as I can tell—but it's changing. I'm not thinking the way I used to think. I can feel it most strongly when I'm reading. Immersing myself in a book or a lengthy article used to be easy.... Now my

concentration often starts to drift after two or three pages.
I get fidgety.[1]

Me too.

But there are some signs that the problem isn't as bad as
we think—or at least the problem is different from what we
think. According to an article in the *New York Times*, there's not
much evidence that attention spans are actively shrinking.
Psychological tests that measure attention and focus haven't
shown much change in recent decades. What's changing,
according to the research, is our *motivation* to pay attention.
When we're motivated to focus, we will. But the prevalence of
technology is giving us myriad ways of indulging the pinball
game inside our heads. So it's not that, say, factory workers
during the Industrial Revolution had more focus than we do,
but that they had a lot less pulling at them—fewer tempta-
tions and distractions.[2]

So maybe we're not too far gone.

But our emotional lives are also taking a hit. In her
now-famous TEDx talk, author and researcher Brené Brown
chronicles the many ways we try to crowd out negative emo-
tions, to keep ourselves from experiencing tough feelings.
We work too much. We eat too much. We reflexively pick
up our phones and scroll, text, tweet, and play games. But
there's just one problem with that strategy, Brown says, and
it's a big one:

> You cannot selectively numb emotion. You can't say, here's
> vulnerability, here's grief, here's shame, here's fear, here's
> disappointment. I don't want to feel these. I'm going to
> have a couple of beers and a banana nut muffin.... When

we numb those, we [also] numb joy, we numb gratitude, we numb happiness. And then we are miserable, and we are looking for purpose and meaning, and then we feel vulnerable, so then we have a couple of beers and a banana nut muffin. And it becomes this dangerous cycle.[3]

This kind of numbing is everything that an improvised life is fighting against. If improv is based on paying attention and being present, then a scattered mind and a numb heart are going to get in our way.

∗   ∗   ∗

Psychology tells us there are at least two kinds of attention—and both are vital in life and in improv. *Hyper* attention is perhaps the more ancient type. We evolved as a species to be on the lookout for threats and sudden movements around us so we could outrun predators and other dangers. According to Duke University professor N. Katherine Hayles, "Hyper attention excels at negotiating rapidly changing environments in which multiple foci compete for attention." We use hyper attention when playing soccer or waiting tables. Teachers need hyper attention all day long in the classroom.

The other type of attention is *deep* attention—the ability to follow a complex thought to its conclusion: to think deeply, to question our knee-jerk assumptions, to remain unswayed by sound bites. "Deep attention … is characterized by concentrating on a single object for long periods (say, a novel by Dickens), ignoring outside stimuli while so engaged, preferring a single information stream, and having a high tolerance for long focus times," writes Hayles.[4]

We need both hyper attention and deep attention to make it through the day. Hyper attention keeps us from burning the eggs while signing our child's permission slip, and it keeps us alert during our commute (which is why texting and driving is so hazardous). Once we get to work, deep attention is what allows us to compile the quarterly report, write the white paper, or debug the computer code.

The best improv incorporates both hyper attention and deep attention. Hyper attention notices the small sigh from a scene partner that provides key information about the character's emotional state, or the movement from another improviser who's about to jump into the action. Deep attention means thinking about the who-what-where of the scene. Have we established how these characters are related to each other? What's happening? Where is the scene headed?

To see hyper attention and deep attention in action, we need look no further than Jesus, who was a master at both. In the Gospel of Mark, Jesus is going about his business when an official named Jairus comes to him: *Will you please heal my daughter?* We don't know where Jesus was headed, but he improvises a response: he changes course, not focused on the future, but attentive to the situation right in front of him.

But then he gets interrupted again, this time by a woman who's suffered from a flow of blood for twelve years. She walks up to Jesus from behind and touches the hem of his robe. It's not clear whether she sneaks up behind him out of a sense of shame or out of a sense of confidence that even this tiny bit of contact will be enough. But she is healed immediately.

Jesus notices her touch right away. He has the hyper attention to feel the "power" flow from him to her. He then shifts to deep attention as the woman tells him her whole story. One imagines Jesus listening, unhurried, while the rest of the crowd is eager to move on to the next whiz-bang healing or exorcism. He hears her whole story, calls her "Daughter," and praises her faith.

In the next moment, it appears that Jesus does two things at once. According to Mark, *while Jesus is still speaking to her*, he hears Jairus's friends tell him that his little girl has died, and to give up on disturbing the teacher. Having heard this, Jesus shifts his focus to Jairus: "Do not fear, only believe." He is present with the woman—deep attention—and *also* hears what's going on around him—hyper attention (Mark 5:21–43).

As someone who walks through life pretty scattered and inattentive a lot of the time, I try to write off Jesus's actions here as the work of a master: *I can never be that attentive.* But I suspect that in this story, Jesus is showing us what full humanity looks like. Jesus is present, fully inhabiting his life.

*   *   *

Improv can seem like a fast-moving art form, and much of the time it is. But it also has slow moments. When TJ and Dave begin their improvisation together, they often stand in silence, watching one another. They aren't in their heads, trying to think of something to say. They're very externally focused. They're sizing each other up with openness and curiosity: *How is he standing or walking? What's the expression on his face? What clues are there? What gifts is he giving me that tell me who our characters are to each other, and how can I Yes-And that?*[5]

It's not unlike the attentiveness we bring to the beginning of a romantic relationship, when even a person's quirks and foibles fascinate us. It's the awe of staring at a newborn baby. It's the moments of beautiful clarity and all-rightness with whatever we see in the moment. The Christian language for this is *kairos*, a Greek term for "holy time" or "God's time," when the moment feels full of wonder, joy, and grace.

As I type these words, I'm painfully aware of how much I miss on a daily, hourly basis. *Kairos* passes me by all the time, like the commuters on the Washington, D.C., Metro some years ago. They had no idea that the man playing in the L'Enfant Plaza station was master violinist Joshua Bell.[6]

Lately, for instance, I've easily fallen back on a noncommittal "hmm" or "yeah" when my kids are talking. They notice it too, and they've started calling me on it. I used to try to fake my way through, but they're getting too old for that. So these days I make an effort to stop what I'm doing, turn to them, and own it: "You know what? You didn't have my full attention before, but now you do. What did you say?" Improv practice has been teaching me to pay attention and to be humble enough to admit when I've missed the mark.

*   *   *

Improv as an art form has an immediacy that makes it a powerful analogue to life. There's no rehearsal for a future performance. There's no script. There's no backlog of work that shows a progression of technique or intent. There are only the performers onstage, and maybe a chair or two. It can be scary to be so unflinchingly *there*.

Veteran improviser and comedian Chris Gethard points out that when players get nervous or anxious, they start talking about a character offstage who's not in the scene. Or they describe something that happened in the past or will happen in the future, rather than what's going on right then and there.[7] In my beginners' class, we fell into a lot of scenes in which we planned stuff. One night we ended up with scene after scene that centered on an upcoming trip to Six Flags. I don't know why Six Flags kept coming up, but everyone was trying to get there. Family vacation. Band trip. (Bachelorette party?) The problem was, we spent so much time planning to go to Six Flags that we never made it to the dang amusement park. Boring—onstage and in life.

We all know what convenient hiding places the past and the future can be. As a runner, the hardest thing in the world for me is to stay in the current mile. During every long race, I start to agonize midway through: If I'm a little tired now, imagine how I'll feel at mile 20! I call it "pre-fretting." So I've adopted a series of mantras: One good mile. One good minute. One good block. The unit of time doesn't matter; what matters is bringing energy back to the present. Stay here. Be now. That's an improvisational impulse.

Some years ago, during an Easter sermon, Pope Francis referred to Jesus as the "everlasting today" of God.[8] I don't really know what he meant by that, except that Jesus focused on the here and now. Unlike many contemporary Christians, who focus on getting to heaven and helping others do the same, Jesus kept the focus on the present by saying, "The kingdom of heaven is at hand." Or "among you." God's reign is right here, right now, while many of us are looking over the next rise.

My teacher at Second City, Liz Joynt Sandberg, has a great definition of a good improviser. It's someone who's "relentlessly present in space and time." It's that simple, and that hard.

Chapter 12

See Defeats Differently

When I developed a stress fracture while training for a marathon a few years ago, my doctor recommended cross-training while I recovered. Anything that wasn't weight-bearing would be fine, he said—elliptical, biking, and swimming, for example.

I wasn't thrilled. I had no access to an elliptical machine. Biking was tedious in my hilly Virginia neighborhood, and I'd never really gotten the hang of shifting gears. And swimming? Even swimming in a pool often made me nauseous, thanks to the famous McKibben motion sickness that had kept my siblings and me off cruise ships and roller coasters for much of our adult lives.

I groused. "If I wanted to do those other things, I'd be doing them already." But I was more concerned about losing the level of fitness I'd gained from diligent marathon training, so I decided to give them a try.

Swimming was the easiest to start with, but it was a rocky go. Even the relative calm of a swimming pool was enough to make my stomach do backflips after ten or fifteen minutes. Turning my head from side to side to breathe certainly didn't help. But I found a few centering phrases that helped calm my anxiety, and I learned what kinds of food quelled the nausea. And each time I swam, I was able to go a few minutes longer.

Two months later, a friend put a home elliptical machine up for sale, and the price was right.

A few months after that, a friend offered me her road bike for free—all I had to do was make the two-hour drive to pick it up at her house in Pennsylvania and take care of a few easy repairs.

You might know where this is going.

Since coming back to running, I've started competing in triathlons, in which participants swim, bike, and run. I feel stronger than I've ever felt because I've diversified the exercise I do. And it wouldn't have happened without my running hiatus.

I stop short of saying I'm glad I got injured. It's a bridge too far to say a broken body is ever a good thing. Still, it gave me an opening to improvise. An improviser learns to see defeats with new eyes, to be attentive to unexpected opportunities even when things go terribly wrong. Now I'm an amateur triathlete as well as a runner.

$$* \qquad * \qquad *$$

This chapter is a perilous one to write. We can't do the work of making meaning for one another—each of us has to do it for ourselves. Some tragedies deeply defy any convenient, tidy reframing. And too much damage has been done by religion offering silver linings, hastily woven together and smothering the deep questions of life.

I can only say that sometimes, with eyes wide open and clutching Yes-And, we can peer through a tiny hole in the rubble and muse, "I wonder what would happen if I poked it just like this?"

About fifteen years ago, the great jazz musician Wynton Marsalis performed a rendition of Victor Young's ballad from the 1930s, "I Don't Stand a Ghost of a Chance with You." Marsalis performed unaccompanied, and according to David Hajdu in *The Atlantic*, it was a wrenching, masterful performance. Right at the climax of the song—terrible luck!—someone's cell phone rang, a cacophony of electronic noise. The spell broken, the patron making his walk of shame to the exit, Marsalis paused for a moment—but only a moment.

Then he replayed the cell-phone ringtone, note for note. And he began to improvise on it, making variations on the tune. Slowly, the musical spell was cast again, and the audience returned to him. He changed the key, slowed the tempo … and then, incredibly, picked up exactly where he left off in the song.

Without the interruption, the audience would have heartily applauded the virtuoso performance. But thanks to the interruption and Marsalis's graceful way of embracing it, the ovation was tremendous. He had heard the obstacle with gracious ears and responded with his best Yes-And.[1]

That's the vision of a true improviser. It's a hopeful orientation—turned always toward possibility.

What would it mean to be oriented toward the hopeful as a default—in other words, to assume first that there must be a Yes, and then to look for it? Some of us are naturally oriented toward pessimism—and I'm one of them. When something goes awry, I'm a champ at catastrophizing. The plan isn't just off the rails; it's The Worst Thing That Could Have Happened. This takes a special kind of skill—in fact, I'm pretty sure I read an article that says pessimists are more creative than optimists. (I may be making that up, but don't tell me otherwise. It's my story and I'm sticking to it.)

Still, catastrophizing doesn't make for good improv, whether we're performing onstage or living life. Catastrophizing keeps us fearful, suspicious, and stuck. Instead, I've been challenging myself to experience my life with a different orientation. Hope means there's always another Yes to pursue. As poet Wendell Berry advises, "Be joyful though you have considered all the facts."[2]

✶   ✶   ✶

We may want to diminish the Wynton Marsalis story, to say that's all well and good, but what happens when life hands you the worst heartbreak imaginable?

I'm writing this chapter by the light of a candle lit for my friend Lisa. Lisa is sitting with her son Ted, who's clinging to life after a terrible drug reaction. There's no longer any hope for Ted to recover. Yet the family waits for matches to be found so Ted's organs can be recovered and donated to people who need them. Because that's what we do. It's the best Yes in this inexpressibly terrible circumstance. As I ponder having the vision to see a way forward through tragedy, Lisa's candle illuminates the words I write, reminding me that this work can be excruciating.

Sheryl Sandberg, an executive at Facebook, experienced the anguish of her husband's sudden death while they were on vacation. In an instant, Sandberg became a young widow with two small children at home. Since then she's had to learn how to live within a life that doesn't look anything like what she'd planned.

A few weeks after Dave died, she says, "I was talking to my friend Phil about a father-son activity that Dave was not here to do. We came up with a plan to fill in for Dave. I cried to him, 'But I want Dave.' Phil put his arm around me and said, 'Option A is not available. So let's just kick the s--- out of option B.'"[3]

You may bristle at the profanity, but I find it energizing and honest. Finding the Yes-And amid horrible circumstances and the death of Plan A is defiant and stubborn: *We're gonna make something redemptive out of this mess.*

It's important enough to repeat: the meaning each of us makes from the experiences of our lives is ours and ours alone. I'll stand in the way of anyone who tries to connect the dots for anyone else. But either way, life hands us our share of disappointments, failures, and dashed dreams. And as Sandberg told an audience after her husband's death, "It is the hard days—the times that challenge you to your very core—that will determine who you are. You will be defined not just by what you achieve, but by how you survive."

A noisy interruption.
A broken bone.
A devastating loss.

When the unexpected happens, our reaction is often compounded by a sense of shock—*I did not see that coming.* Such a shock is unsettling, and it can lead us to facile explanations about God's plan. Everything happens for a reason, we tell ourselves; we just don't know what it is.

I don't believe our defeats and tragedies are by God's design. They're by-products of randomness, human frailty, and free will that make up the world we live in. But even if there were a plan, what would it matter? At every moment, the question is, *Now what? What's our next move?* An improvising God calls us to see what we can see—the situation right in front of us, no matter how surprising, annoying, or downright deplorable—and find the best Yes-And possible.

Principle 4

Find Your Troupe

Heroes didn't leap tall buildings or stop bullets with an outstretched hand; they didn't wear boots and capes. They bled, and they bruised, and their superpowers were as simple as listening, or loving. Heroes were ordinary people who knew that even if their own lives were impossibly knotted, they could untangle someone else's. And maybe that one act could lead someone to rescue you right back.

—Jodi Picoult, *Second Glance*[1]

Improv is rarely a solo endeavor. So who's on the journey with us? Who are our best improv partners—the ones who Yes-And, who listen to our contributions, who respond in a spirit of playfulness and curiosity?

And who are the improvisers we wouldn't necessarily have chosen—the ones who drive us crazy and push all our buttons? How can we learn to improvise at our highest level with these scene partners as well?

Chapter 13

Play Well with Others

Bob and Kelly stepped forward and looked at each other. After a moment, Bob balled his hands into fists, licked them, and rubbed them on his face.

From my comfortable place observing from the back line—not in the scene itself—I deciphered his motions instantly. As a lifelong cat owner, I know what it looks like when a cat washes its face with its paws. I was impressed: *A non-human character! This should be interesting.*

Kelly looked at him for a long moment. It was clear she had no idea what he was doing. *No cats at home*, I thought—or maybe her brain froze onstage, which happens to all of us from time to time. She began mirroring his movements—always a helpful strategy in improv when you don't know what to do. Then she spoke.

"You're right. Rubbing the ice cream cone on your face is really great!"

For an instant, Bob was taken aback—we all saw the shock flicker across his face. *Wow, did she read* that *wrong. Now what?!*

And then—because this is what you do in improv—he went with it. In an instant, he pivoted from being a cat taking a bath to being a person who smeared ice cream on his body.

"Well, I find that the cream and sugar are great for my complexion, and the chocolate chips make a nice exfoliant."

Delight! This silly scene became one of the most memorable moments from that class. Afterward our instructor said, "I loved the way you two kept gifting each other, building on what the other person offered, which obviously wasn't what Bob had in mind going in." Although the scene started with a misunderstanding, that quickly became irrelevant—what mattered is that Bob and Kelly stuck with it and created something together that neither could have done alone. Rather than become defensive—*How could she not know I was being a cat?!*—Bob accepted the detour from his plan and decided to follow the adventure for a while. And it was ridiculously glorious.

The cat-cone scene reminded me how often we bring our assumptions and experiences to the "stage," convinced that others will understand exactly where we're coming from. *How could they possibly see things any other way than mine?* And when a misinterpretation occurs, we're faced with a choice: we can dig in our heels and fight to keep our original assumptions in play, or we can get curious about the new direction: set our agenda aside, go along for the ride, and see where we go together. Maybe we don't have it all figured out. Maybe the other person has something to teach us.

Despite improv's reputation as an anything-goes art form, there are boundaries and standards that keep people feeling safe and supported. Every improv theater I know has its own set of norms. For instance, James Dwyer, a teacher at the Upright Citizens Brigade in New York City, hands out a set of group rules to his classes, explaining, "If it's on the sheet, it means someone has hardcore broken it before."[1]

But assuming a basic level of safety and a willingness to be curious—why not? Why not loosen our grip just a little? As author Wade Davis puts it, "The world in which you were born is just one model of reality. Other cultures are not failed attempts at being you; they are unique manifestations of the human spirit."[2] Davis is speaking anthropologically, but his statement is true for individuals too. There may be no bigger adventure on earth than exploring the terrain of another person's mind and heart.

∗   ∗   ∗

When you join an improv class, you never know who's going to show up. In my first class, I was older than everyone else by about twenty years; two people were still in college. I was also the only one who was married with children. The millennial-heavy group would routinely head out for drinks following class, while I'd hightail it to the Metro for the hour-long ride back to the suburbs and a five o'clock alarm the next morning.

This generational divide presented challenges. We often played a warmup game in which people took turns jumping into the middle of the circle and singing a song. Everyone else had to sing along with gusto—even if we didn't know the words, we had to fake it, and fake it BIG. (BIG generally makes for stronger improv.) But my knowledge of popular music waned around the time I graduated from college, before some of my improv classmates were even born. I didn't know any of the music my millennial teammates were singing.

And I loved it.

I've also been in classes with people who were much like me—married with children, similar in age, and so on. (And, sad

to say, the spaces where I currently improvise are very white.)
It's comforting to speak a common cultural language, but
something about that first class was particularly energizing. My
classmates didn't think like me, and their cultural references
were completely different than mine. Ultimately I learned more
and was stretched in ways I couldn't have predicted, because I
had to break out of familiar ways of thinking and meet my fellow
improvisers on their own terms.

In his book *The Wisdom of Crowds*, James Surowiecki explores group dynamics and reveals that, generally, large groups
of people can be wise (i.e., knowledgeable) in ways that may
surprise us. Consider the game show *Who Wants to Be a Million-
aire?*, in which contestants were asked questions and would
poll the audience for responses. The audience got the answers
right more than 90 percent of the time, because the crowd was
diverse enough to cover all the bases. A group is a lot less wise,
Surowiecki says, if everyone comes from the same race, class,
age, or other demographic category.[3]

Happily, the things that make for a wise crowd (according
to Surowiecki) also make for invigorating improv. A diverse
team means a much broader base of experience to work with.

Unfortunately, we now live in a world of echo chambers,
in which it's possible to read only those web sites and news
sources that reinforce our own point of view. Powered by hidden algorithms, our social media networks curate what we see
to the point that we can get insulated from alternate perspectives. That's why it's more important than ever to be connected
to people who are different from us—they burst our bubbles
and help us understand people who come at life differently.
We're all in this together—as communities, as nations, as a
planet. We need the wisdom of the crowd.

*   *   *

Technically, it's possible to improvise by yourself onstage. But why would anyone want to? Improvising with others makes things messy and unpredictable, as Bob and Kelly showed us. But it also makes our jobs so much easier. Instead of doing all the work ourselves, we get to play off the energy and experience of others.

I met Janine in one of my classes at Second City. A teacher, she had never taken an improv class and was eager to do well—so eager, in fact, that she would step onstage, let her partner get out a sentence or two, and then launch into a two-to-three-paragraph monologue that was often hilarious but left us all exhausted on her behalf. She wasn't trying to dominate; she just let her enthusiasm get the best of her. Mercifully, our teacher let her off the hook: "Janine, you're working too hard here. Improv is way easier than you're making it, because it's not all up to you. Let the other people in the scene help you, and then you can help them in return."

I was reminded of *Bull Durham*, one of my favorite movies, when veteran catcher Crash Davis tells the arrogant rookie pitcher to stop striking people out. "Strikeouts are boring. Besides that, they're fascist! Throw some ground balls—it's more democratic."[4] In other words, let the team be the team. In improv, as in life, everyone should get to play.

It's how God made us—one for another. In Genesis 1, God has fashioned the universe, piece by piece, heavens and earth, sky and sea, and pronounced it all good. Quasars, good. Conifers, good. Manatees, good. In Genesis 2, technically a second creation story, we learn for the first time that something's not good: "It is not good that [the human] should be alone; I will make him a helper as his partner." Dinosaurs and dandelions, black holes and bobcats—the creation isn't good without relationship. So God offers up animals of all description, in hopes of finding the one who will be a suitable partner to Adam.

I'm always struck by the fact that God gives Adam veto power in this story. God doesn't impose on Adam: *Here's your partner. Like it or lump it.* God defers to Adam in a way that's relational. God doesn't compel. Adam, for his part, honors God's creation by naming this menagerie God creates, and when God fashions Eve—made from the same stuff as Adam, yet her own person—Adam says, *Yes, this is the one.*

Remarkable. The God who created everything is also collaborative and non-coercive. Relationship is at the heart of God's nature. Christians are stuck with a strange math when it comes to God: the doctrine of the Trinity says that *one* God is known in *three* persons, traditionally described as Father, Son, and Holy Spirit. How is this possible? How does 1 = 3? The finer points of that calculus will be left to other theologians for now. But I remember the delight that rippled across our class in seminary when we learned the Greek word *perichoresis*. It's hard to define precisely, but it helps describe the sense of mutuality between the three persons of the Trinity. There is no hierarchy, which means that the Holy Spirit, who's often a bit player in discussions about God, is just as vital to God's nature as the Father. *Perichoresis* implies a dynamism, a "dancing around" rather than a fixed, static reality. The three persons of God relate to one another in a constant dance of grace.

This kind of God—dynamic, yet consisting of discrete persons—is exactly the kind of God who creates us for relationship, and who sees fit to improvise with us.

Chapter 14

Be a Pirate, a Robot, or a Ninja

I've played with all kinds of people in class and onstage, and there are some who blow me away with their creativity and talent. I marvel at the stuff they say and do, and I think, *Where does that even come from?*

Over time I've learned that there are different types of improvisers, each with their own natural abilities and gifts, and we need them all. Long-time improviser Billy Merritt calls them pirates, robots, and ninjas.[1]

The pirate is the one we probably think of when we imagine an improviser. She or he is the zany one, the one who comes in with guns (or one-liners) blazing. The pirate is fearless and unpredictable, offering a scene lots of big, powerful gifts. A pirate is willing to go for broke in order to get a scene going, and is willing to risk bombing in order to do it. John Belushi, at his most Belushi-est, was a pirate.

Improviser Lisa Kays is a therapist who sees these categories through the lens of psychology. She connects the pirate to Sigmund Freud's work on the id, the part of the brain that oversees the instinctual impulses. A pirate can be pure id: if it feels good, if it provokes a reaction, do it. But too much pirate energy can be overwhelming. "The audience at first has fun,"

Kays writes, "but then becomes confused, even tired, as so much is happening, so fast, and it's all so big that they can't keep up. There is no narrative plot to rein it in, to tie it together, to give it meaning."[2]

That's where the robots come in. These are the logical ones who keep bringing the scene back to reality. They provide grounding for the action, not to squash the fun but to heighten it. When a scene has some connection to reality, we can better relate to it. This connection gives the scene humor and pathos. Robots may not always get the biggest laughs—though as the straight man or straight woman, they often do—but the scene would fly off into space without them. Their guiding concern, according to Merritt, is to respond honestly to what's going on: "What is my character, and how would he or she react truthfully to this?"

According to Kays, "In some ways, the robot is the provider of safety in the scene, and, perhaps, in relationships. Pirates, if left unchecked, can be dangerous to themselves and others. Robots are, potentially, the partners and friends who help rein [pirates] in, gently point out the consequences of their actions, and remind them to take precautions." She sees the robot as an expression of Freud's ego, working with tools of reason to bring the scene back to earth.

Then there are the ninjas. Ninjas do small, subtle things to help scenes along. They may drop in for a quick walk-on that provides energy and material, or relocate the action to another setting when the scene is stalling, called a "cut-to." Ninjas also end the scene when it runs its course, which is called "editing." (In long-form improv, editing is achieved when one player runs across the front of the stage between the audience and the players, like a curtain sweeping closed.) They draw little

attention to themselves because they have no ego. These players sneak in and out of scenes, doing the little nips and tucks
that make them better. Kays sees the ninja as akin to Freud's
superego—controlling the impulses of the id and keeping the
ego focused on greater norms and expectations.

Once I learned about these three types, I began seeing
them everywhere, not just in improv. Many ensembles, in
fact, feature these three types. One friend suggested that John
Lennon and Paul McCartney were the pirates of the Beatles,
the prolific songwriting engine that gave the band its creative
energy, but was also a source of volatility. Ringo Starr was the
easygoing robot who kept things going and grounded. And
George Harrison was the stealthy ninja genius who didn't
jockey for the limelight but who contributed brilliant musical flourishes in a less flashy way. ("While My Guitar Gently
Weeps," anyone?)

Or consider the TV show *Parks and Recreation*. Andy Dwyer
(Chris Pratt) is the classic pirate—always willing to do something crazy, like wear a bandana in lieu of underwear. Leslie
Knope (Amy Poehler) is less zany, but very much a pirate—she
provides the manic, can-do energy around which the show
revolves. Ron Swanson (Nick Offerman) is the straight-man robot—playing off other people in the scene, responding to what's
going on, providing commentary. And April Ludgate (Aubrey
Plaza) is a scene ninja—she can do more with three words or a
sideways glance toward the camera than just about anyone.

The best improvisers are able to inhabit all of these
personas, but most players instinctively gravitate toward
one of them as a natural fit. Myself, I'm not a pirate by default. Maybe it's a matter of confidence and experience, and
with time that gift will come. As a pastor, I've often been the

idea-generating pirate, so improv gives me a chance to follow others' lead onstage and let someone else drive the action for a change. My temperament is well-suited to being a robot—I like thinking about the internal logic of a scene—but I enjoy the ninja role the most. It's like conducting music: listen for the crescendo of the big laugh, then cut the scene. Slip in, do my thing, and leave.

Big, pirate-y laughs are fun, but in improv, what matters is the scene. Our responsibility is always to the scene, to the whole. "If the whole body were an eye, where would the hearing be? If the whole body were hearing, where would the sense of smell be?" The Apostle Paul asks these questions in 1 Corinthians as he locates roles for each person in the larger body of Christ.

I try to remember the scene, the whole, whenever I'm tempted to be jealous of a fellow improviser's gifts. I remember being in one group that stood with mouths agape whenever one of our members got going. His contributions were so off-the-wall, so thick and juicy with stuff to work with. It was easy to despair—I'll *never be like that*—but our instructor always snapped us out of it. "Stop wishing you were him. We've already got one of him. Now we need you to be your best you."

*　　　　*　　　　*

So far in these pages we've looked at Jesus as a master of improvisation. What about his friends and followers? What kind of improvisers were they? I like to ask church groups, "Who was Jesus's best pirate?" And many groups answer instantly with one voice: *Peter.* Peter is always full of grand gestures. When Peter sees Jesus transfigured on the mountain, he wants to go right to work building dwellings so they can stay up there and bask in that wonderful feeling. When he tries to rebuff Jesus for washing his feet, and Jesus chastises him, he changes his tune: OK, Jesus, *wash my whole body instead!* And when the disciples are fishing together after the resurrection and see Jesus standing on the shore, three guesses about which one of them jumps into the water and swims out to meet him.

And the "robot" disciples? One can imagine several of them on deck, shaking their heads at the dog-paddling Peter, saying, *Buddy. Pretty sure we can get there in the boat.* In the Gospels we meet Martha, a no-nonsense robot, providing hospitality in her home for Jesus and his followers. Matthew, the keeper of the purse, is like Martha. In improv, we don't mean "robot" in the sense of cold and emotionless. Instead, robots are the ones who do the indispensable tasks to keep the ministry going: surveying the crowd for five loaves and two fish; fetching a donkey for Jesus to ride into Jerusalem; and, in the days of the early church, preaching, healing, and serving the community.

Robots aren't necessarily the stars of the show. But the way of Jesus isn't created with grand, Peter-esque gestures. It is built through countless ordinary moves toward grace and wholeness. The Christian movement simply wouldn't have survived for two millennia without the robots.

As for ninjas, I like to make a case for Thomas. Thomas doesn't have a starring role like Peter, and he doesn't provide the vital organizational structure of the behind-the-scenes robots. Instead, Thomas steps into the narrative right when we need him. In the Gospel of John, Thomas is the one who wants to go to Bethany to tend to Lazarus, who's gravely ill. The others want to keep Jesus far away from there—tensions are beginning to boil, and it could be dangerous—but Thomas is ready to go: "Let us also go, that we may die with [Jesus]" (John 11:16). It's a "cut-to," a classic ninja move in improv. When a scene is stuck in neutral, a ninja senses it and changes the location with a single statement: *Cut to Bethany.*

And Thomas, most famously, is the one who doesn't see the risen Jesus right away, and who is skeptical of the resurrection. He demands to see Jesus with his own eyes. This, too, is a ninja move—an instigating move not focused on Thomas's own glory but on drawing out evidence of the risen Christ: *Show me what you've got, Jesus.* And Jesus does.

∗   ∗   ∗

Think about the people in your life. Who are the pirates, the robots, and the ninjas? If you're part of a religious community, consider the makeup of your governing council or leadership. What's the balance like? We need pirates, the ones with lots of creative energy who generate countless great ideas. But if we have nothing but pirates, we may have issues with follow-through, or feel exhausted by the welter of worthy projects—more than we could possibly implement. The robots are the doers, the people who accomplish things, who keep the lights on and the food pantry stocked. These are the ones who make sure tradition is observed and details are tended. The place would fall apart without them—but too many robots without enough pirates can get stuck in "the way we've always done it." As for ninjas, these folks keep a low profile—they don't say much in the committee meeting until there's a logjam. That's when they speak up, making the statement or asking the question that gets everything unstuck.

Now think about your personal life as if it's a movie, and you're watching the opening credits roll. Do you have the cast you need to tell the best story possible? Yes, some folks are in your movie whether you'd want them there or not. But think about the others. Do you have enough pirate friends, the ones who're always up for an adventure and who never fail to make you laugh? You need them to keep your life from getting stale. And what about robot friends? They're the ones who'll be there for you no matter what—always available to listen and lend a hand. And don't forget ninja friends—the ones who have a knack for knowing just when you need a "thinking of you" phone call or text message.

Now think about the ratio of these people you know. Do you have too much of one, maybe not enough of the other? How might you create a better balance in your film—your one and only life? Remember—you get to be the casting director.

Chapter 15

Serve One Another

In his book *The Age of Missing Information*, author and activist Bill McKibben (no relation) undertook an unusual experiment: he asked a cable company for videotape of every program, on every channel they broadcast, for an entire 24-hour period. Armed with some 1700 hours of video, he retired to his home in the Adirondacks to watch it all. It took him a year. His reflection on that experience forms the backbone of his book.

Of all the varying messages, sales pitches, and narratives McKibben experienced during this immersion, there was one that rose to the top: "The residual idea, the central theme, is that each of us is the center of the universe—the most important thing on earth. We're being told we're the heaviest object around and that everything needs to orbit around our ideas of convenience and comfort."[1]

What's in it for me? This question is the engine that drives our consumer-oriented culture. We are each our own god, cajoled and seduced into having it our way, searching out that elusive cure, product, or relationship that will fill whatever needs we may have.

McKibben's experiment took place in the 1990s, and I'd be interested to see what's changed in the texts and subtexts of media in the twenty-first century. While the content of our programming is quite different—fewer soap operas, more reality TV; fewer jokey sitcoms, more sardonic dysfunction—I suspect the central theme would be the same. Each of us is still "the heaviest object around."

Consumerist messages are so powerful because they play on our own sense of fear and anxiety: we don't have enough, we don't do enough, we *aren't* enough. Social media deepens this anxiety by introducing a creeping sense that everyone else knows how to "adult" better than we do with happier vacations, better-behaved kids, and healthier gums. And the latest spate of dystopian movies and television heightens our anxiety even further, leading us to wonder whether the very fabric of society is unraveling.

And yet, as singer-songwriter Carrie Newcomer likes to remind us, the things that have always saved us are still here to save us: kindness, generosity, community.[2] But these things require a focus on the other. They require us to set aside "what's in it for me" and listen for that steadily beating heart, present in so many of the world's finest religions and philosophies, in which serving others is the highest ideal.

If our focus is only inward, we become organisms curved in on ourselves. By serving one another—as improv encourages—we can save our own lives.

*　　　*　　　*

Improviser and author Patricia Madson breaks down three different ways of observing and analyzing the circumstances of our lives.

In the critical mode, we focus on everything that's wrong

with the situation. The critical method is all about the self: my judgments, my opinions, and my agenda.

In the scientific mode, we strive to see the situation as objectively as possible. The self and the other are meant to disappear—what matters is the objective truth of the situation. Madson argues that the scientific mode is largely an illusion because we can never fully remove ourselves and our own biases from a situation. And if we're talking about the mysteries of human interaction and relationship, would we really want to? We're inevitably part of the mix.

In the improviser's method, we look for the gift in the situation, the Yes-And we've been exploring throughout this book. Madson elaborates, pointing out that in the improviser's mode, it's not the self that matters most, and it's not about removing self and other. In this mode, it's the other that looms large. What gift is the other person offering me, imperfectly and maybe unknowingly? And what gifts can I offer back that would support and love that person the best I can?[3]

Earlier I wrote that the job of improvisers is to serve each other in the scene—good improvisers are fundamentally team players rather than solo showboaters. Put in philosophical terms, a good improvisation is one in which the We is more important than the I. This orientation requires mutuality, compassion, humor, and risk.

I remember a game during a Second City class in which each of us was to come forward and dance in a silly, exaggerated way, while the rest of us mirrored that person in both motions and intensity. During the game I noticed a couple of people mimicking the motions, but only in a halfhearted way. I felt the energy in the room start to flag, but I also felt reluctance well up inside me. *There's no way I'm going to step forward. What if they don't like my dance? I'll embarrass myself!*

I was grateful when our teacher noticed this halfheartedness. She yelled out, "What are you doing? Your job is to protect the freak! They put themselves out there, and you're too cool to follow their lead? Coolness kills improv. Just stop."

I realized, or perhaps remembered, that it wasn't the front person's job to come up with a worthy dance. It was the group's job to affirm, to support that person, and in fact to *make the dance worthy* by virtue of their wholehearted commitment to it—which is really a commitment to the person, the relationship.

"Protecting the freak" means that when someone steps out and takes a risk, we don't look with eyes of judgment but respond with support, which is our own risk-taking move. In doing so, we create a perpetual-motion engine of courage.

Coolness kills improv, but it kills a vibrant life too. Coolness is detached. Coolness is judgment. It's the reason many of us have traumatic memories of adolescence, because that's when we learned to judge things on the cool scale, even as we ourselves were judged on those terms and found lacking. As human beings, we're wired for love and acceptance. When we take a risk—when we dance in front of a group, or say yes to the blind date, or apply for the job we're 100 percent excited about but only 70 percent qualified for—we count on our community to share our enthusiasm and have our backs. In improv, we're also called to be those people.

∗   ∗   ∗

I often talk with groups who want to hear more about improvisation as a life practice. They're perfectly happy to talk about it, safely and anonymously, around tables, but they'd rather die than get up in front of others and do it themselves. It's always a fun challenge to figure out how to get reticent, serious-minded folks out of their seats and playing in sync with each other. I've got one secret weapon I use, and it's never failed me yet.

It comes out in a game called "What are you doing?" One person starts miming an action—playing putt-putt golf, for instance. Another person comes forward and asks, "What are you doing?," and the first person names something completely different than their actions suggest. So instead of "I'm golfing," they might say, "I'm baking a cake." The second person accepts the offer and starts baking a cake, and the first person is done and can sit down. Then a third person comes up, and the game continues with a new suggested action.

Here's a game that never fails to get people out of their seats. Why? Because people realize very quickly that if they don't come forward, their friend whose dignity they care about will be stuck up there playing putt-putt golf for the rest of his life. In fact, I've heard group after group describe this as "rescuing" each other. These reserved people will get up and pretend to hopscotch or ride a pogo stick or even give birth if it means getting their friend off the hot seat.

This is the way we're made. We'll do things for each other that we'd never do on our own. My friend Leslie recently spoke at a fundraiser for a health-related organization that has helped her family. She isn't a public speaker—in fact, just the idea of it fills her with dread. But when the organization asked, she knew she had to say yes. That's how it works. When we care enough about the people involved, we strive to overcome concerns about our own comfort. My friend did exactly that. With a strong but emotion-filled voice, she gave words to her experience and urged the audience to support the organization.

$$*\qquad*\qquad*$$

I often have groups do an exercise in which each person draws a simple doodle on a piece of paper: a squiggle, a zigzag, whatever strikes their fancy. Then people pass these doodles to the person on their left, so everyone ends up with a different sheet of paper. The task is to create something with it, to build on the gift that's been given and to make it their own—to make it something new.

I remember a workshop in which an older woman completed a doodle that was passed to her by a ten-year-old girl. I loved what they created and asked the woman if I could have it. Without hesitating, the woman said, "Well, let me ask my drawing partner." She then turned to the ten-year-old and asked if she was OK with letting me take the drawing home. That was exactly the right impulse. The drawing didn't belong just to the woman; it was a collaboration between the two of them.

As we build our tribes, our troupes, we know some people are a part of our lives whether we like it or not: a grumpy neighbor, a nasty co-worker. But we can also surround ourselves with people who will help us create the best Yes-And possible. And what gets created—whether it's a doodle, or a scene on stage, or a day in the life—is a partnership between pilgrims on a journey together.

Find the Right Structure

Once upon a time...
And every day...
Until one day...
And because of that...
And because of that...
Until finally...
And ever since then...

If you analyze many stories—the stories that really last over generations and across cultures—they follow some version of the above structure. These phrases are also part of an improv game in which groups make up a story by taking turns completing the statements.

Improv, too, has a structure. Sometimes the energy can seem frenetic and devil-may-care, but good improv also has an underlying logic and progression. Humans thrive on structure, but too much and we feel restricted. Principle 5, "Find the Right Structure," explores the power of boundaries and planning—yes, planning!—and how to find the right amount of organization to free up your creative energies for the work of improvisation.

Chapter 16

Get Lean

Base … Hit.
Hit … Man.
Man … Hole.
Hole … Jump.

It's a simple word-association game. One person says a word, and the next person says the first word that comes to mind, and so on around the circle.

The first time I played this game was a disaster. Every time it came around to my turn, I locked up. My conscious mind took over and I stammered, trying to think of a "good" response. We'd been told not to worry about the words making sense—I knew that wasn't the point of the exercise—but I couldn't help myself. The more I told myself "Just say anything," the more my brain shut down. I might as well have said, "Make sure your response is in Urdu." I had nothing.

In the next round, the instructor started a rhythm by slapping her knees twice, then snapping her fingers twice. We were told to say the words in rhythm and to continue the game around the circle, not breaking the rhythm. *Great. This is going to be even worse,* I thought.

But, like magic, my tongue loosened up. Each time a word came to me, I was ready with a response—not necessarily a good one, but something that kept the momentum of the game going. And having that rhythm made all the difference.

It seems like the first round, when I had plenty of time to think, would have yielded the best result. But give someone all the time in the world to come up with a word, and they'll thumb through their mental dictionary, weigh options, and compare. We often think constraints create anxiety and paralysis. But give people two slaps and two snaps, and they'll bypass their conscious mind and respond quickly so as not to break the rhythm. For me, and for many of the groups I've worked with, it's the right amount of structure to keep the game going.

Ashley Goff, a pastor who does a lot of improvisation with her Washington, D.C., congregation, likes to say, "Structure promotes safety." Her church has been known to do all kinds of creative liturgy in worship—from painting watercolor responses to Scripture using the water in the baptismal font, to bringing in a big pile of compost for a service focused on God's call to care for the earth. Church of the Pilgrims is a vibrant, creative place, full of people who are interested in something different than church the way it's always been done.

Still, change can make even the most adventurous people uncomfortable. What makes these experiences successful, even amid the discomfort, is that there's enough structure present to give people a safe place to stand. What the congregation does is the result of careful planning and collaboration with a wide range of church members—it's not done on the fly, though they do adjust to the unexpected circumstances that arise. Ashley and her colleagues on staff serve as competent and caring guides for the worship experience. And the relationships forged within the congregation provide their own sense of structure and belonging. "I'm not sure about compost on the sanctuary floor," a skeptical churchgoer might say, "but I know and trust the people here, and I know they'll be with me as I experience this."

In Chapter 14 we talked about robots and how important they are to good improv. What robots do is connect us with norms, traditions, or an underlying narrative. These underpinnings are a vital ingredient in rich improv. As Samuel Wells writes, "Improvisation can't work without a tradition. Try improvising without a tradition and you dry up within 30 seconds."[1]

* * *

Healthy, life-giving structure seems to be God's mode of being as well. Genesis 1 shows us a God who creates all that is, and does so with a fundamental logic. Days one through three are about creating spaces: light and dark, waters and sky, sea and dry land—boundaries and delineations. Then, in days four through six, God returns to each of the domains of the first three days and populates them. On day four, God stitches the sun, moon, and stars into the curtain of the heavens. On day five, God flings the birds into the air and scatters the animals that swim in the waters. On day six, God fashions the creatures of the land, including human beings. Then comes day seven, the day of rest. In this story we see the kind of God the Bible illuminates again and again: a God who creates order out of chaos.

The structure of this story suggests a theological purpose. The story was collected and written down at a time when the people of Israel were experiencing exile in a foreign land, under a foreign power. Everything they knew about the world had shifted and been destroyed. The very ground under their feet was unfamiliar, even hostile, to the way of life they'd known and celebrated in their homeland. From where would their hope come? It would come from God, who made heaven and earth. What the people needed, and what the creation story provided, was a defining myth, a master story of a God who had made all things with order and purpose, and who lived in relationship with God's people. The creation story brought a sense of orientation into a disorienting experience of exile. This creative God knows that structure creates safety.

$$* \qquad * \qquad *$$

So how much structure is the right amount? Too little structure can leave us rudderless, as my experience with the first word-association game shows. But too much leaves us feeling burdened and stuck. In their book *Simple Sabotage*, Robert M. Galford, Bob Frisch, and Cary Greene talk about the ways that organizations take on too much structure unconsciously, in ways that squelch creativity and innovation. The insistence that ideas go through "channels," for instance, can be a sabotaging maneuver. Other structural creativity-killers: referring items to committees (where people secretly hope they'll go to die), reopening matters already decided (nothing kills the energy in the room faster), and bickering over the wording of things (well, nothing kills energy faster except for this).

Sometimes organizations inherit burdensome structures that simply don't fit anymore. Several years ago I was called to a small congregation as its solo pastor—about forty to fifty people attended worship each week. When I arrived, I asked for a copy of the church's organizational chart. I was handed a piece of paper that had eleven committees on it. Eleven—for forty people! Needless to say, most of these committees had been dormant for a long time. Meanwhile, the church kept itself running just fine, serving its neighbors in various ways. I realized that part of my job was to help the people of the church look honestly at how they were *really* organized, apart from how they felt they *should* govern themselves. And over time we moved to a leaner, more team- and task-based approach.

L. Gregory Jones proposes a number of remedies for innovation-killing structure. These include storytelling that focuses on our mission and purpose, rapid innovation with an eye toward constant improvement, and improvisation—specifically, a Yes-And mentality.[2] Strong organizations, whether companies or churches, constantly work to find the right structure for optimal functioning. The leaner, the better.

*   *   *

But what about individuals? What kind of structure gets us "lean" enough to improvise well? These answers will vary from person to person. One person's color-coded calendar is another person's organizational straitjacket. Take dieting, for instance. There's a popular 21-day program that involves filling up containers with various kinds of foods—proteins, vegetables, and grains. For some people, it injects the perfect amount of structure into their eating. For me, it's too restrictive—I feel stymied by the lack of flexibility. (Plus, there's no container designated for cookies.)

One thing all of us can do to create more energy for other tasks is to offload decisions that aren't that important. President Obama was famous for wearing suits in just two colors: navy and gray. And he rarely deviated from these two, because the leader of the free world has more important things to worry about.[3] This principle scales for ordinary folks too. I'd rather devote my time and creative energy to writing a blog post or an article than to managing my wardrobe, which means I stick to a fairly boring "uniform," especially when working from home.

When we do have decisions to make, our natural preferences can set us up for good improv, or they can hinder us by bogging us down. In his book *The Paradox of Choice*, Barry Schwartz, a professor of social theory at Swarthmore College, talks about two kinds of decision-makers: maximizers and satisficers. Maximizers make a purchase or major decision by finding the optimal choice after a careful and exhaustive search.[4] These are the people who subscribe to *Consumer Reports*, do detailed analysis, and comparison shop. I'm married to a maximizer, and I can vouch for how useful it is, because if my husband recommends a home appliance or vacation lodging, I know it's the best possible choice given our constraints and preferences.

The downside is that maximizers can take a long time to decide things. They can also overthink their decisions. When we're shopping for a new car, doing as much research as possible makes good sense. But when it's date night and I'm hungry for sushi, my maximizing spouse can inadvertently gum up the works. He loves finding the best place in town given our budget and location, so he's scouring Yelp while I'm standing in the doorway with my coat on. Sometimes I just want sushi.

But then, I'm a satisficer. When satisficers find a product or outcome that fits their criteria, their search is over. It doesn't matter that there may be something even better out there that fits their standards—once satisficers find something that checks all the boxes, they're done.

Schwartz argues that we're all satisficers to some extent. We can't spend our whole lives looking for *the* best cardigan—at some point we have to say, "This will do." But he also argues that people who are able to satisfice are happier than maximizers. They're more content with "good enough." Maximizers tend to feel anxious, worrying that they missed an even better option than the one they so carefully chose.

True confession: like me, Schwartz is a satisficer. So of course he's going to see his perspective as the preferred way to be. I'm not willing to judge which one is better. But I do want to suggest that improvisers rely on satisficing a lot. When I say the first thing that comes to mind in a word-association game instead of holding out for something better, that's a satisficing move. Forward momentum, not precision or cleverness, is key to keeping the action going. "Good enough" is the gold standard for improvisers, and a lean, flexible structure helps us get there.

Chapter 17

Take One Small Step

Andy Weir's 2011 novel *The Martian* isn't just an entertaining story. It may be the best fiction book about improv in the last decade. Astronaut Mark Watney comes to consciousness after a terrible accident and realizes he's completely alone, 140 million miles from home. The rest of his crew has left him behind on the surface of Mars, assuming him to be dead. He has no clue how to contact Earth or his crew, or even how to think about rescue.

But none of that matters at the moment because, thanks to the accident, he's got a piece of shrapnel sticking out of his belly.

In such dire circumstances, the next steps become very clear. A rescue plan is pointless if he bleeds to death first, so he's got to deal with his injuries. Once he successfully separates the metal from his person, the next task reveals itself: to assess the habitation facility to see if it's still operable. Once that's done, the next task is to figure out how to feed himself for a long period of time. He still doesn't know how he'll contact Earth, but again, that's a moot point if he dies of starvation. So food comes next: "Okay, I've had a good night's sleep, and things don't seem as hopeless as they did yesterday. Today I took stock of supplies . . . ," he writes in his log.[1]

Watney's story is infused with improv, because he's got to figure out a way forward amid radically altered circumstances than he'd planned for, often with equipment that was intended for a completely different purpose than it must now perform. For example, the hydrazine normally used in rocket fuel can be burned (very, very carefully) to make water. But even more broadly, the story shows improv in action through the way Watney goes about these tasks: by doing the next right thing, however small. First, immediate medical crisis. Next, shelter and food. Next, communication. Bit by bit, he improvises his way forward.

As the novelist E. L. Doctorow famously said, "Writing is like driving at night in the fog. You can only see as far as your headlights, but you can make the whole trip that way."[2] Whether we're building a novel or an improv scene or a life (on Earth or on Mars), we don't need to know how it's all going to turn out. Which is good, because we *can't* know. But by taking the next step, we'll get there.

✳   ✳   ✳

I've been in countless improv classes in which the instructor gives directions for an exercise and then says, "OK, start."

And we all stand there.

Finally someone jumps in and gets the action going, and it's always a welcome relief. It doesn't matter if the contribution is especially clever. What matters is setting something in motion. Over time I've decided that, whenever possible, I'll be the person in the improv group who's willing to go first. I have lots of things I'd like to do better as an improviser, but one thing I can do is be willing to volunteer first. And whatever might come out of my mouth—some of it good, some of it not so good—my stepping forward always feels strong and brave.

Sometimes in life, we wait too long for conditions to be just right—we want to have thought through all possible outcomes, completed all our research, and have the facts safely flanking us when we jump. Research and thoughtfulness are good things. But they can also be stalling tactics. Nothing moves forward until we step out and act.

Many of us have had to take giant leaps of faith in our lives. But in daily life, these giant leaps are seldom required. Instead, we need to negotiate the baby steps of faith. They're no less important than a leap, because baby steps start things. And baby steps take their own kind of courage.

In the TV comedy *Friends*, Monica and Chandler are planning to get married when Chandler gets hit with that clichéd condition afflicting so many sitcom characters: cold feet. Ross finds Chandler hiding out on the big day and says, OK, *let's not even think about getting married right now. Let's do something small. First step, you take a shower. That's not scary. No big deal, right?*

Then, after the shower, Ross says, *How about putting on a tux? You've worn a tux before. Easy.* And, step by tiny step, Ross gets him ready.

Eventually Chandler says, OK, *what's the next step?*

And Ross says, *You get married.*[3]

It's good for a laugh, and yes—even with baby steps, sooner or later there comes a point of no return. But even getting married is a series of small steps. Take a deep breath. Walk down the aisle. Repeat after the officiant. Promise to love one's beloved tomorrow and the next day and the next. Marriage is a lifetime of baby steps—brewing the cup of tea in the morning, letting the petty grievance go, grasping hands when the doctor delivers the news. Love is faithfully expressed in small acts of service as much as in grand gestures.

A few years ago I decided to keep a journal for each of my three children. I don't trust my memory to recall their Halloween costumes, or when they lost their final tooth, and I thought they might want to know these details someday. So I bought a notebook for each of them where I could record memories. I've undertaken tons of projects like this in my kids' lives, only to abandon them: my closet is stuffed with half-finished knitting projects, and the less said about their baby books, the better. But this practice has persisted. Why? Because I required myself to write no more than one sentence at a time in each book. I knew that if I demanded more, the task would become overwhelming, and I would eventually stop doing it altogether. (And I still go months without touching the books sometimes.) But I also try to write ordinary things in them rather than waiting for the big headlines, because life is built on these small moments.

There's a wise saying at Second City: "Bring a brick, not a cathedral."[4] When we're improvising with others, we don't arrive with a fully formed scene and plunk it down. We each show up with one piece, and together we build.

Bringing a brick takes away the pressure to come up with something elaborate as a prerequisite to play. We're free to jump into the improvisation if we're long on enthusiasm but short on plan. Besides, our own prefabricated cathedrals are rarely as lovely as the things we construct in community. What we create collectively will probably be better, and even when it's not better, it's more authentic. It's more collaborative. It represents the group of us working together. Maybe we're not meant to build a cathedral at all. Maybe we're meant to build a bridge, or a lifeboat.

*   *   *

Many years ago, writer Courtney Martin undertook a study of young activists to see what motivated them to keep going amid disappointments and the slow rate of change. In her twenties at the time, she was trying to figure out her own contribution to making the world better, and nothing seemed "big enough": "How did they get up, day after day, and face the heartbreak, the losses, the absence of glory? How did they measure success? How did they know their work mattered?"

During this exploration Martin met Raul Diaz, a caseworker for men serving prison sentences for serious crimes. He called himself a "re-humanizer": he confronted the inmates with a generous dose of tough love, holding up a mirror to their crimes and challenging them to view their victims with empathy.

In a world that values scalability, in which bigger must be better, Diaz and other activists demonstrated a different reality. "Raul knew his work mattered, not because it scaled," Martin wrote, "but because it transformed one life, then another. He would lose one, then save one. Lose another, save another one. Sort of. Over time. Depending on your definition. He knew his work mattered because he kept looking these guys in the eyes and telling them that they deserved good lives, that they were capable of goodness, that he cared about them, unconditionally."[5]

Diaz understood the importance of changing one life at a time. In monotheistic tradition, both the Talmud and the Quran say, "Whoever saves one life saves the entire world." Christian Scripture doesn't put it quite so plainly, but Jesus says that when we reach out to serve the "least" among us, it is as if we're serving Christ himself. And he often spoke about the kingdom of heaven being present in small things—a wee bit of yeast, a tiny mustard seed, granules of salt. Jean Vanier is the founder of the L'Arche communities, which nurture people with mental disabilities and those who care for them so that together they can live in dignity and tenderness. "A community," Vanier says, "is only being created when its members accept that they are not going to achieve great things, that they are not going to be heroes." He continues, "Community is only being created when they have recognized that the greatness of [humanity] is to accept [our] insignificance ... and to thank God for having put in a finite body the seeds of eternity which are visible in small and daily gestures of love and forgiveness."[6] Those daily gestures of love and forgiveness are the bricks we bring to this work of improvisation.

Chapter 18

Plan Right

Improvisation has an underlying structure. That structure may be subtle and spacious, but it's there, and it involves several key elements:

Taking a Yes-And approach.
Establishing the who-what-where of the scene.
Choosing honesty over cleverness.
Emphasizing the importance of relationship.
Ending the scene on a high note.

Similarly, a life created improvisationally needs structure, sometimes even a plan. But what kind of plan?

When my husband and I were preparing to have our first baby, our childbirth educator often told us, "Worry is the work of pregnancy." Instead of trying to pacify us with platitudes about how everything would turn out all right, she encouraged us to think deeply about the various scary scenarios. She said, "OK, what if you do need an emergency C-section? What happens then? What if your child has to go to the NICU? How will you handle that? What questions do you have, what resources do you need, so you can meet that challenge head-on?"

And then she helped us get the information required to face those scary outcomes.

By "worrying" over possible scenarios, we began to think through how we would respond if they came to pass. This process may sound nerve-wracking, but it turned out to be empowering. Instead of relying on positive thinking as some kind of good-luck charm—*Everything will be fine*—we decided to expect the unexpected and ready ourselves as much as possible.

As it turns out, the worst-case scenarios we envisioned didn't happen. We had a healthy baby. But labor brought unexpected twists and turns, including a couple of complications that made my recovery slower than expected. These complications weren't on our list of possible events, but by thinking through lots of potential outcomes, I had more confidence to handle whatever might happen.

The truth is, we're not in control of our lives, and the unforeseen happens. Plans fall through. People get sick. Marriages end. The plant closes down. Loved ones die. Our job as improvisers is to use our resources to put together a life in the wake of these things—maybe not the life we had planned, but a good life, a life with dignity, fashioned out of what's on hand.

That does involve some planning on our parts, but not necessarily plans per se. As President Eisenhower said, "Plans are nothing; planning is everything."[1] Improvisers don't take the stage with a plan. But they've been through a process of "planning": they've trained, analyzed scenes, improved their proficiency, gotten to know their team, and practiced. Good planning doesn't anticipate every possible outcome. Instead, it's a process of building skills so we can weather the surprises.

When Mark Watney finds himself stranded in *The Martian*, his survival is a feat of ingenuity and imagination—rationing, repurposing, and recalculating at every turn. But Watney had trained. He had prepared for scenarios one through a thousand, so when scenario 2,253 happened, he had some tools at his disposal. Similarly, an improvised life doesn't emerge fully formed. It's not Athena, sprung from the head of Zeus, suited up and ready for battle. It's Jesus, born a human baby and formed over a thousand experiences, encounters, and learnings, so that when the decisive moments occur, he's ready.

Samuel Wells writes, "When people say, 'Life isn't a rehearsal,' I say, 'But it is, really, isn't it?' Life is a rehearsal … [and] the habits of rehearsal are everything we do in life.… Most of my life is preparation for crucial moments. I'm not saying I've reached a defining moment in my life, but I've reached some fairly crucial moments where I had to act from memory."[2]

Religious communities may recognize the movements of worship as a kind of rehearsal: we sing familiar songs and pray customary prayers so when challenges arise and we don't have our own language to put around them, we can rest in the words of our faith traditions. Christians pass the peace of Christ with a handshake or a hug so we remember to be the presence of Christ for people we meet in everyday life. We put money into an offering plate so generosity can become a habit, as automatic as breathing.

$$* \qquad * \qquad *$$

The first time I ever ran a half marathon, the signs held by people in the crowd kept me going when I wanted to quit. ("You run better than the government." "Worst Parade Ever.")

My favorite, though, was "Trust Your Training." When I decided to train for a full marathon, I took that sign to heart and found a training plan that was well respected for getting new marathoners to the starting line, healthy and prepared.

And I attacked that plan with everything I had. As a rule-following good girl, I was in heaven. The plan told me when and how far to run, and I complied. In return, I felt assured that I would be successful. *Trust your training.*

Everything was going well—until four weeks before race day, when I hurt my back after hoisting my recalcitrant preschooler during a meltdown in the drugstore. It took me a couple of weeks to get back to running, and by then, it was almost race time. My longest run had been eighteen miles, well short of what the plan prescribed.

"How can I trust my training when my training has let me down?" I asked a friend a few weeks before the race.

"Just make a new plan," she said.

"Wait—what?"

"Make a new plan," she repeated. "A plan that involves you running eighteen miles. Which you've already done. It's like putting something on your to-do list that you've already done, just so you can cross it off."

It was a trick I played on myself, and it worked. I arrived at the starting line, healthy and feeling prepared, or at least prepared-ish. (I offer this approach to other type-A control freaks like me. If it's too scary to ditch the plan altogether, make a new plan that matches what you end up doing, and call it good.)

But, more importantly, I realized that I'd been treating my plan as a security blanket, a hedge against the unexpected: *If I jump through this set of hoops, everything will be OK.*

A plan isn't a security blanket. Rather, every plan we undertake, like my training plan, is about preparation. My training was about creating good habits, building strength, and learning about myself and what I was capable of. It was about setting an intention and building actions toward that intention.

*   *   *

Whether we're training for a marathon or planning to have a baby, the journey has a set outcome we're hoping to reach. But life isn't always so linear. Sometimes having a plan, even a loosely drawn one, can limit our own abilities, keeping us locked into one particular path.

Several years ago, psychologist Saras Sarasvathy undertook a study of successful entrepreneurs. She conducted long interviews with some forty-five businesspeople, all of whom had at least fifteen years of experience launching companies and taking at least one of those companies public. She expected to find a bunch of goal-oriented achievers who put plans together and followed them with focused precision. What she found was the exact opposite.

Oliver Burkeman writes about Sarasvathy's research in his book *The Antidote: Happiness for People Who Can't Stand Positive Thinking*:

> We tend to imagine that the special skill of an entrepreneur lies in having a powerfully original idea and then fighting to turn that vision into reality. But the outlook of Sarasvathy's interviewees rarely bore this out. Their precise endpoint was often mysterious to them, and their

means of proceeding reflected this.... Almost none of them suggested creating a detailed business plan or doing comprehensive market research to hone the details of the product they were aiming to release.

Instead, what these successful entrepreneurs had on their side was a sense of flexibility, "not merely about which route to take towards some predetermined objective, but also a willingness to change the destination itself." Burkeman specifically invokes the language of improv when describing these business leaders.[3]

These entrepreneurs seem to have the ability to place themselves in what photographer Dewitt Jones calls "the place of most potential"—to keep their eyes open to possibilities off the known path.[4]

The good news for improvisers, of course, is that all places have some potential. And any planning we do should have potential, rather than product, in mind. Our tasks are to build resilience and skill, to trust our training and to worry well, so we can face those things we never could have anticipated.

Chapter 19

Make Peace with "Not Enough"

Improv shows often begin with a group of players, a couple of chairs, and a word from the audience.

That's it.

It never seems like enough, yet improv always happens.

I once took an improv class that had about ten members. Our time together culminated in a showcase with other improv classes. As the day of the showcase drew near, members of our class started announcing conflicts with the date. They were all important reasons to bow out—a son's award ceremony, a mother receiving chemotherapy—but they accumulated at an alarming rate for the ones left behind. By the end, there were four of us. Four newbie improvisers, instead of ten.

I sent my teacher a panicked note: How could we do this with so few people? Could our group's TA join us, at least, so we had a little more safety in numbers?

She replied reassuringly but firmly: "It'll be fine." She spoke with the confidence of someone who knew from experience that fears over not having enough are common—and can often be the fuel for something fantastic.

The night of the showcase came, and the four of us gamely showed up. Wonder of wonders, it turned out to be one of the most invigorating evenings I've had onstage. I can't speak to the quality of the improv—though we did get a lot of laughs—but I can say that each of us was fully invested in giving our absolute best and supporting everyone else. There was no hanging out on the back line, wondering if someone else would initiate a scene. If we felt the impulse to jump in, that was our sign to just do it.

When we finished our set, we dashed offstage, high-fiving each other, relieved but also ecstatic. What started as an experience of "not enough" became a great victory. Our teacher seemed thrilled, but unsurprised: "You guys pulled this off with only four people. Now you can do anything."

*   *   *

When we're faced with a difficult situation, we often approach it with an eye toward what's lacking:

If we had just a little more time.

A little more money.

A few more people.

A few more resources.

A little more support for our project.

This sense of deficiency can leave us feeling stuck and give us convenient excuses not to move forward. Yet scarcity fuels improvisation.

People often ask me about my writing practice. How do I set up my life? What rituals do I put in place? Do I have a specific time I write each day? Do I have a dedicated writing space? The answers are "Not well, Very few, No, and No." I admire people who have a daily writing time they never violate, but my life feels too chaotic for that. Like Virginia Woolf, I long for a room of my own—except the best I can manage is a corner desk in the basement next to the treadmill. Sometimes I write on the couch. Occasionally I'm at the library. On Wednesday afternoons I'm in the car, in a shady parking spot, while my daughter attends her cello lesson. At least right now, that's the way it is.

Like many aspiring writers, I read articles about the daily habits of great authors (Hemingway wrote every morning; Stephen King writes ten pages a day[1]), and many of them seem so ... civilized. The chopped-up bits of time I have make it hard for me to think deeply. But if there's an upside, it's that I've made peace with the random periods of time in the margins of my day, and I've learned how to focus relatively quickly. I have a friend who has a talent for being able to fall asleep anywhere, no matter how loud or uncomfortable the place. I guess I've learned to write anywhere—mostly out of necessity.

*   *   *

Phil Hansen is an artist who began his career interested in pointillism—applying numerous small dots in patterns to make a larger image. His focused pursuit of this art form resulted in a tremor in his hand that made drawing dots impossible. So he'd grip the pen harder, which only increased the shaking. Eventually he was diagnosed with a neurological problem that he himself had made worse by holding on so tightly. He was devastated, wondering if his art career was over. As he was leaving his doctor's office, the doctor shrugged and said, "Maybe you should embrace the shake."

Ultimately, he did—he found other ways to create art besides pointillism. A working artist today, Hansen also speaks to groups about embracing limitations as a source of creativity. He describes his experience of finally having enough money to buy art supplies and going hog-wild at the store. He came home, excited to create, and ... nothing. He felt blocked. He was surrounded by his myriad supplies, yet the unlimited options they gave him left him feeling stuck. He needed more structure in which to work.

This experience led him on a quest: to see if he could create using less than a dollar's worth of art supplies, for example. He started by making drawings on donated coffee cups. Then he began creating art that would end in its own destruction. He made a sculpture of Jimi Hendrix with 7,000 matches that he then lit on fire, and an image using frozen wine that disappeared as it melted.

Hansen concludes, "Embracing the shake for me wasn't just about art and having art skills. It turned out to be about life, and having life skills. Because ultimately, most of what we do takes place here, inside the box, with limited resources. Learning to be creative within the confines of our limitations is the best hope we have to transform ourselves and, collectively, transform our world."[2]

$$* \qquad * \qquad *$$

I'm an avid fangirl of *The West Wing*—I've watched the series several times and return to it often as mental comfort food. One of my favorite scenes involves President Bartlet preparing for a debate. He asks to wear the same tie he wore in a previous debate—back then, he'd spilled something on his planned tie, and his aide Josh Lyman gave him his own tie at the last minute. He did well in that debate, so Josh's tie became his lucky tie.

Unfortunately, the cleaners have ruined the lucky tie, so he has to go with a regular one for the upcoming debate. He knows it doesn't matter—or *shouldn't* matter—but he laments its loss anyway. "There was a lot of juice in that tie. It was like in the last seconds, just the energy getting me out onstage," he explains to his wife, Abbey. She gently mocks him: "Do you think there's any point in going on with the debate?"

But just as he's walking out the door to go onstage, Abbey says, "I feel bad. I don't feel like I've done enough to prepare you for this debate"—and cuts off his tie off with a pair of scissors.

"You're insane!" he shouts, while she cackles to herself, dangling the severed tie in his face. As the countdown to go onstage continues, he scrambles to find Josh and borrow his tie—in effect creating a new lucky one.[3] Scarcity to the rescue! Bartlet doesn't spend the last few minutes making sure he's memorized the answer to the question about trade with China—instead, he gets a powerful shot of adrenaline, a key ingredient in kicking butt and taking names. The tie scramble takes him out of his head. It's a perfect example of what I call "playful scarcity": putting limits on yourself to see what you're capable of.

Leonard Bernstein liked to say, "To achieve great things, we need a plan and not quite enough time."[4] Too much time, or even adequate time, will leave us wedded to the details. We can cross off all the steps and think that it's the plan that saves us, that makes us successful. But not enough time means we need to improvise. We may end up throwing things overboard that we once thought were indispensable.

I think about the preachers I know who, every week—barring vacation or other circumstance—climb into a pulpit or walk onto a stage with some kind of prepared sermon, whether they typed it out, or jotted down notes, or planned a note-less sermon. Every week.

How many sermons would be completed if we preachers had all the time in the world, if our congregations said, "Go ahead and let us know when you want to call a worship service together. Whenever it's done will be fine"? Real life would conspire against us every time, not to mention the headiness of trying to preach the word of God. Yet the sure knowledge that Sunday is coming drives us to our laptops, our desks, or the big table at the coffee shop. Preachers complain about the relentlessness of Sunday, but I'm not sure many of us would get the words down otherwise. An enforced deadline imposes scarcity upon us, thus spurring creativity.

∗   ∗   ∗

While everyone deals with a feeling of "not enough" from time to time, not all scarcities are equal. Too many people in the United States and around the world live in a state of real scarcity, without access to adequate food, water, shelter, or education. Too many worry about making ends meet, having to weigh whether to make the car payment or pay for the prescription essential for one's health. There's nothing playful in that kind of deprivation.

Yet learning to improvise our lives means that each of us, regardless of our privilege or scarcity, has a personal agency that cannot be taken away. Each of us can choose how to respond to our own lives—and that choice is ours and ours alone. In the end, if improv has anything to offer us, it's a way of understanding that choice, which is ours regardless of circumstance. Whatever life hands us, we can find the Yes and seek the And. We can make the most creative choices possible within the constraints in which we find ourselves.

That doesn't mean we accept inequality in our systems as the way things should be. Part of finding the best Yes is to make that Yes as inclusive as we can. And if life—like improv—is oriented toward serving others, we must care for those in our communities, so that their Yeses can be as rich and as life-giving as possible.

Principle 6

Live More Deeply

Being obvious is . . . a demonstration of faith, an embodiment of disciple-ship. Being obvious means trusting that God will do what only God can do, and thus having the freedom to do what only the disciple can do.

—Sam Wells, *Improvisation: The Drama of Christian Ethics*[1]

We may think improv consists of a series of off-the-wall moves. But going for the unpredictable sometimes means we're trying too hard. Much of improv is based on doing the next right thing—which often leads us to deeper and deeper levels of honesty and humanity.

Chapter 20

Wrestle with The Voice

"I'm not an artist."

"But I don't know anything about acting."

"I can't do that."

In my work with groups, I sometimes ask people to draw something on a sheet of paper or get up in front of others for a simple improv exercise. Nobody is ever required to participate. But it's always a little dispiriting (though maybe not surprising) when people refuse with the excuse that they're not "good" at it. I never asked them to be. I never asked them to be anything but who they are, willing to do something a little different than what they're used to.

By the time we reach adulthood, we've endured a couple of decades of wanting to appear competent and cool. Propriety has firmly set in. We'd rather die than be put on display for others' judgment or scrutiny. That sounds like an exaggerated statement, but fear of public speaking is near the top of people's lists of phobias, higher than drowning or flying in an airplane.[1]

What do we sacrifice for the sake of our propriety? Second City answers that question with a quote from Amy Poehler, emblazoned on the entrance to its training center: "No one looks stupid when they're having fun."

Many of the most interesting adults I know, the ones I admire, are quick to pick up the crayons, volunteer to go to the front of the workshop, wear the outlandish tie, or learn to scuba dive. They're on a lifelong journey to unlearn the unhealthy lessons that attach themselves to us during our early years.

Part of that unlearning is coming to terms with The Voice: the internal critic who keeps a running commentary on what we do, unhappily judging our efforts.

"The only thing I don't want to watch onstage is you apologizing or hesitating," Liz Joynt Sandberg likes to say to her classes. Every class I've taken has been guided by that ethic. Yet apology and hesitation are the default modes for many of us when we're faced with something new. That's the work of The Voice chattering in our ear.

The Voice, also called the censor, is guided by two overarching sentiments: "You're not good enough" and "Who do you think you are?" These sentiments stop us mid-risk and keep us safe on the beaten path rather than in the improvisational mystery, which is scarier, but ultimately more interesting and satisfying.

Resistance comes in many forms, and it's nothing new—it's been a part of our earliest faith stories. When God challenges Moses to lead the people of Israel out of slavery in Pharaoh's Egypt and to the Promised Land, Moses tries to rebuff him: "I don't speak well." Gideon makes a similar protest when asked to lead the people of Israel against the Midianites: "My clan is the weakest in Manasseh, and I am the least in my family." Then he comes up with various feats for God to perform to prove God is as real and powerful as God claims to be. Only when Gideon is properly assured does he agree to assume leadership.

Sometimes we shrink from risk because, like Moses, we don't trust ourselves to have what it takes. Perhaps we avoid the challenge because, like Gideon, we don't trust God. Put another way, we are fearful of mystery. We want assurance that if we step out and take a chance, everything will work out all right. Gideon demands proof of God's abilities. And while God's feats of amazement seem to satisfy Gideon, they don't really guarantee a good outcome when he goes up against the Midianites. An improvised life just doesn't work that way.

With The Voice yammering in our ear, trying to bully us back to the safe, predictable path, we can respond in a range of ways. Perhaps we might stop thinking about The Voice as antagonistic—and, in effect, make friends with it. The Voice may be conveying important information if we know how to decipher it.

Ira Glass, longtime producer of the radio show *This American Life*, understands The Voice in this way. Glass says that each of us has a sense of our own personal taste—what kind of work we find excellent and compelling, whether it's a poem we write or a scene we create onstage or the perfect apple pie or an effortless jump shot. When we're first getting started in a creative endeavor, there's a huge gap between our expectations and our abilities. "A lot of people never get past this phase; they quit," Glass says.

I'm not an artist.
But I don't know anything about acting.
I can't do that.

But that discomfort itself, that gap between The Voice's vision and our reality, is a sign to keep going, says Glass:

> Most people I know who do interesting, creative work went through years of [the gap]. We know our work doesn't have this special thing that we want it to have.... And if you are just starting out or you are still in this phase, you gotta know it's normal, and the most important thing you can do is do a lot of work. Put yourself on a deadline, so that every week you will finish one story. It is only by going through a volume of work that you will close that gap, and your work will be as good as your ambitions.[2]

For Ira Glass, the censor isn't a bad judge of quality. It's a very good judge, in fact, because the censor is ourselves. So the trick isn't to silence The Voice. The trick is to keep going despite The Voice's telling us we're no good ... and maybe retraining that Voice a little. It's healthy for The Voice to be our North Star, pointing us toward our destination. It's less helpful for The Voice to wield a yardstick, tut-tutting at how far we have to go. In the end, all of us are works in progress, trying to find our way. That's why even the most experienced improvisers play in the attitude of the novice, because there's always more to discover about the art form, and themselves.

Adam Erbrecht is an elementary school principal in Virginia. At his school, they discourage the children from saying they "can't" do something. Instead, they say, "I don't know how to do that yet." "Can't" is a closed system. "Yet" means there's more to uncover.

∗   ∗   ∗

Maybe your Voice is so caustic that you just can't make friends with it. If that's the case, try another strategy. One way to blunt the impact of The Voice is to make sure we're focused on the right things. TJ and Dave, master improvisers, don't step onstage with a goal of being entertaining. "To us, improvisation does not mean being funny. It means being human—or better yet, just being." When they feel themselves getting anxious—when The Voice tells them "This isn't good" or sends other self-defeating messages—they know they need to get back to their central mission. For TJ and Dave, being human in improv means going for what's truthful. "The goal is to be honest, not because it's better, though it is, but because it's easier."[3]

What's our work? If we figure out what our work is, The Voice often takes care of itself. The poet William Stafford wrote a poem a day. When people asked him how he pulled it off, he said, "I lowered my standards."[4] He understood what his job was: it wasn't to write a good poem. It was to write as much as possible—to show up for the work.

And showing up for the work is a direct assault on "You're not good enough" and "Who do you think you are?" Those are statements about being. But rolling up our sleeves and taking action is about doing. And nothing silences the censor like action. The Voice can say "You're not an artist" while we're in the very process of making art, but its protestations won't be credible. Because there we are, doing it.

Spiritual writers like to talk about how we're human beings, not human doings. It's true that many of us get stuck in cycles of activity and need to learn to be still and reflective. But as improvisers, we *are* human doings. We are what we do—not what we say we'll do, not what we hope to do someday. I'm not interested in whether you consider yourself an artist. I'm interested in whether you pick up the colored pencils.

Sometimes our job is simply to trust our own contribution as unique. I wrestle with this all the time. My Voice likes to tell me that the ideas rattling around in my head aren't original at all—that everyone's had these thoughts before, and expressed them better. Patricia Madson addresses this in *Improv Wisdom*: "Do what is natural, what is easy, what is apparent to you. Your unique view will be a revelation to someone else."[5]

✳   ✳   ✳

If all else fails, keep The Voice at bay by playing Beat the Clock—get to work faster than The Voice can keep up. Improvisers frequently step into a scene before they know what they're going to say. They do this because they know that if we can keep two steps ahead of The Voice, it's much harder to hear.

Here's a little-known fact about The Voice: it likes to sleep late. I'm convinced this is why many people write in the morning: the censor's too groggy to offer commentary. I myself can't write in the morning. But I do run at five a.m. a couple of times a week. I do it to get it out of the way, but also to outrun The Voice. I don't fit the stereotype of a runner: I picked it up in midlife; I'm pretty slow; I don't have the traditional runner's body. And with so many things on my plate, running feels like an indulgence I don't have time for.

If I let my intention to run see the light of day, all those objections would take over. So I go stealthily, in the dark, before The Voice has had her coffee and warmed up her vocal chords. And I go with friends, so if The Voice manages to hunt me down, she'll be drowned out by sounds of laughter and friendship—and occasionally, mutual misery. Many people say to me, "It must take so much discipline to run early." For me it's the easiest time, because it's too early to tell myself I shouldn't.

If we're trying to live creative, improvisational lives, The Voice will always be with us. We'll never reach a high enough level of competence—in which we're pleased with ourselves 100 percent of the time—to silence it altogether. But over time, we can learn to manage The Voice, so that our lives will ultimately speak even louder, and with greater resonance.

Chapter 21

Refuse to Hoard

British and Canadian improv pioneer Keith Johnstone says improv is like walking backwards into the future. "[An improviser] sees where he has been, but pays no attention to the future. [The] story can take him anywhere."[1] When the way isn't clear, we go up into the attic of our memory and experience, searching for something that will help us move forward. We bring it down and incorporate it into our own story as it unfolds.[2]

Several years ago I was asked to write a series of reflections for the season of Lent, the forty days leading up to Easter. It was a tight turnaround, and I wasn't sure I'd be able to make the deadline. But I decided to try, because I figured I had a backlog of old writing—blog posts, sermons, poems, and other noodling—that I could draw from and adapt.

I combed through my "attic," looking for any snippets I could use and edit for the book. In the end I had plenty of material and met my deadline. I walked backwards into the project, arms full of ideas, quilt scraps I turned into something new.

But once I was done with the project, there was very little left. I had picked over the contents of my attic until it was next to nothing but empty boxes under the rafters. I remember submitting the draft and feeling a bit frantic. What if no other words came ever again?

Many writers share this worry. Every book is the last book, every article the final work before the words dry up and the writer is exposed as the one-note fraud she is. My father, who was a writer as well, never seemed to have that worry, or if he did, he'd found ways to get past the paralysis that occurs when there are no words left. "Nature abhors a vacuum," he would say when resources seemed scarce and opportunities few. He trusted that new ideas, possibilities, and projects would rush in to fill the empty space left behind.

Even now, with this book, I'm writing, writing, writing, bringing everything I can in hopes that this work speaks to people. And in the end I know I *need* to have nothing left. I need to throw everything I have into this work, because to hold back is the way to dullness and anxiety. Of all the things my father bequeathed to me—both tangible and not—this lesson may be the most precious: *Give it everything you've got.*

Turns out, Dad may have adapted his mantra from Annie Dillard's *The Writing Life*. (Here's more writerly advice: If you're going to steal, steal from the best.)

> One of the things I know about writing is this: spend it all, shoot it, play it, lose it, all, right away, every time. Do not hoard what seems good for a later place in the book or for another book; give it, give it all, give it now. The impulse to save something good for a better place later is the signal to spend it now. Something more will arise for later, some-thing better. These things fill from behind, from beneath, like well water. Similarly, the impulse to keep to yourself what you have learned is not only shameful, it is destruc-

tive. Anything you do not give freely and abundantly becomes lost to you. You open your safe and find ashes.[3]

It's the same for improvisers. Good ideas don't have much shelf life. It's much better to use them as quickly as possible, before they turn to ashes.

*   *   *

Writing, improv, faith—in the end, all of them are fed by mystery. After Moses speaks out against Pharaoh (despite his initial resistance), he leads the people of God into the wilderness, where they become desperate for food. God obliges, providing a strange, flaky substance that coats the ground each day.

Because the people have been starving, they do what most of us do in a state of deprivation: they collect more than they need, just in case the supply dries up. But the stuff doesn't keep—after a day, it spoils.

In Hebrew the substance is called "manna," and it literally means "What is it?" *What is it?* They eat the stuff for forty years in the wilderness, yet its name never changes. Because the question never quite disappears. God provides nourishment, enough for each day. The people of God are sustained—are fed year by year—by a mystery.

At the heart of good improv is mystery. Even well-respected improvisers talk about their bewilderment at how the scenes come together. "Dave and I never agreed to keep going, keep doing shows," TJ Jagodowski writes in *Improvisation at the Speed of Life*. "We simply agreed not to stop yet. We promised each other that the night we get it right, we quit. We haven't had to worry about that yet."[4]

✳   ✳   ✳

Like many aspects of an improvised life, the instruction to "spend it all" runs counter to much of our culture. Old Testament scholar Walter Brueggemann writes, "The central problem of our lives is that we are torn apart by the conflict between our attraction to the good news of God's abundance and the power of our belief in scarcity—a belief that makes us greedy, mean, and unneighborly. We spend our lives trying to sort out that ambiguity."[5]

Yet the way of Jesus is to give sacrificially—and to receive in the same manner. Jesus's ministry was fueled by the hospitality of friends and supporters who hosted him, prepared meals, and allowed crowds into their homes to hear his message—not because it was prudent or personally advantageous, but because it was the gracious thing to do. And in turn, Jesus gave the best of himself to people in need of wholeness, community, a good word, or simply a decent meal with five thousand of their closest friends. Hoarding has no place in the reign of God.

The greatest commandment, according to Jesus, is to love God and to love our neighbor as we love ourselves. Some people appear to love themselves more than their neighbor, so they hoard what they have. *I need to look out for myself and my kids. I've worked hard for what I have. And how can I be sure these people "deserve" my help?*

Other people find it much easier to love their neighbor than themselves, and as a consequence they give so sacrificially that they're unable to receive the care of others—even when they're hurting. *Oh, I'm fine. I'm not worth your time or concern. Give it to someone more deserving. I haven't earned it.*

Both mindsets come from a hoarding impulse—the idea that there's not enough to go around. And faith, like improv, refuses to live in that mentality.

Many of us live within real scarcities—of time, resources, money, health, power, or energy. Some people try to paper over these limitations with chipper "abundance" language, but that doesn't serve us. The word "enough" comes closer, but it still focuses on the amount we have, tallying it and judging it on some scale, albeit a more gracious one. I resonate with Lynne Twist's ideas of "sufficiency," which she describes in her book *The Soul of Money*. Sufficiency isn't an amount—it's an orientation.

> By sufficiency, I don't mean a quantity of anything. Sufficiency isn't two steps up from poverty or one step short of abundance. It isn't a measure of barely enough or more than enough. Sufficiency isn't an amount at all. It is an experience, a context we generate. Sufficiency resides inside of each of us, and we can call it forward. It is a consciousness, an attention, an intentional choosing of the way we think about our circumstances.[6]

Intentional choice is the work of the improviser. How will I approach my life in the spirit of sufficiency? How will I live within the real constraints of my life? Will I hoard my energy, resources, and ideas in a feeble attempt to insulate myself from disaster? Or will I "spend it all" and trust that more will come?

$*$ $*$ $*$

144

Recently I spent some time with a group on a weekend retreat. During the afternoon we talked about improv and the spiritual life, and that evening the planners put together a game night. They started with a few mixer activities, designed to get people mingling with others they didn't know or usually talk with. These mingling games ended with random groups of people sitting at various tables.

The retreat leaders had brought a large number of board games with them—Scrabble, Yahtzee, Scattergories—and put one of them randomly on each of the tables. Then they told us, "You're welcome to stay where you are and play what's in front of you, or get up and move to a table with a game you prefer to play."

I was excited that our table got Bananagrams—it's one of my favorite games and one that's easy to start playing right away, with few complicated rules or play set-up. As we started playing, I looked around and realized something striking.

Nobody in the room had moved.

Everyone had remained at their table and played the game in front of them.

This is the art of sufficiency—not being constantly on the hunt for something better, but orienting ourselves toward the experience that's right in front of us, with all of its gifts and limitations.

Chapter 22

Reframe Loss and Failure

Musician Herbie Hancock remembers a mortifying moment while playing onstage with jazz legend Miles Davis. The band was hot that night, he recalls, and Davis was in the middle of a solo in the song "So What." Then, out of nowhere, Hancock played the wrong chord. It wasn't just slightly off—it was horrifyingly wrong.

But, to Hancock's amazement, "Miles didn't hear it as a mistake. He heard it as ... something that happened. Just an event.... [It] was part of the reality of what was happening at that moment. And he dealt with it." Davis reproduced Hancock's chord and somehow incorporated it into the solo itself: "Since he didn't hear it as a mistake, he felt it was his responsibility to find something that fit," Hancock says.

"That taught me a very big lesson not only about music but about life."[1]

With Principle 3 we looked at having the vision to see defeats and screw-ups with new eyes—to view ourselves more graciously as we live out of our human limitations. In this chapter we go deeper—learning how to move forward from missteps and defeats with grace and awareness, and to see them as a necessary by-product of an improvising life. This isn't a quick, simplistic sort of moving on. It's tough work, involving muscles we may not know we had. It's incremental, with lots of stops and starts.

✳   ✳   ✳

Different schools of improv handle the language of "failure" differently. My colleague Laura Kelly improvises in Richmond with folks who seek to reframe any mistakes that happen onstage. "What happens, happens," Laura says. "You learn to work with it." This is the Miles Davis approach: *It's a thing that happened.* As a young jazz musician named Jake Falce puts it, "Nothing is wrong. Whatever comes out of your instrument is what comes out. Play it and move on. If you play something you don't like, you're always a note or two away from a note that's in the chord/pattern that you want, so just keep going."[2]

In fact, the human brain is skilled at making sense of disparate events and finding connections between them—mistakes don't always get framed as mistakes, but as something we consciously incorporate into the whole. As improviser and instructor Patrick Gantz puts it, "There are no mistakes in patterns. If a progression builds A, B, C, and Z, 'Z' is not a mistake, it's just something to be acknowledged and made part of the pattern. If A, B, C, and Z, then D, E, F, and Y."[3] It's the Miles Davis method.

Colleague Layton Williams studied at iO Theater in Chicago. There they don't avoid the word but seek to destigmatize it: "Well, that was a failure," they say, "but what better place to do it than here?" Then they either analyze what happened or simply laugh it off. And I've played rhythm and pattern games in which the group was instructed to cheer wildly when anyone broke the pattern, or to run around happily rearranging themselves in the circle. These subtle, playful moves put failure in a completely different context.

Part of my ministry training was to spend a summer in Clinical Pastoral Education, working as a hospital chaplain in a program that included intensive group work with other ministry students and one-on-one meetings with a supervisor. The program was notorious for being an emotional and spiritual meat-grinder. A seminary classmate described it best: "In CPE they figure out what all your buttons are, then push them until they don't work anymore." Learning to improvise uses a similar process, especially as it relates to failure. Mistakes are inevitable. Not every offer is a winner, not every Yes-And a feat of inspiration; relatively few are, in fact. The key is to be prolific enough and relentless enough in making offers and saying Yes-And that we desensitize ourselves to the discomfort of making mistakes.

Given the choice between the perfect action that remains in my head and the imperfect action that's actually lived out, my natural inclination is to choose the former almost every time. But improv doesn't allow for such theoretical perfection—messy reality is always the better course.

*   *   *

Years ago I learned that mastering a skill or a body of knowledge involves four stages of growth. The first is incompetent and unaware—we don't know what we don't know. We're so new at something that we can't even conceive of what we still have to learn. Then comes stage two, incompetent and aware.

This is the most anxious stage, because we know what we don't know. We're painfully aware of the gap between where we are and where we hope to be. Next, usually after a long, painful time spent in stage two, we reach stage three: competent and aware. This is probably the most fun stage, because this is when we perform well—and we know it. Then comes stage four, the spiritual zenith: competent and unaware. This is the level of the sage, in which the skills become second nature and we get out of our own way.

Much of our lives seems to take place at stage two—incompetent and aware. It's not a comfortable place to be. But an improvisational mind-set will help us keep perspective during the discomfort: *It's just an event*. And if we're growing, this cycle will repeat itself again and again. Just when I feel like I know how to parent elementary-age children, they become teens. As soon as I master the latest social media platform, there's something new.

Do we ever complete the stages of growth? If anything, we move deeper into the mystery of not knowing—but perhaps while becoming more at peace with that mystery. I have no idea if I'm a better improviser than I was when I first began. I certainly hope so. But I do know I'm more comfortable not knowing.

And I'm trying to be more like Michelle Jenneke, a competitive hurdler from Australia. She constantly strives to get as close to the hurdle as possible without grazing it, but guess what? You can't do that without falling. She says, "I'm always trying to push myself to go faster and do better and get as close to the hurdle as I can, and when you do that, you hit them.... I really like it when I fall over in training.... It shows me that I'm doing the right thing."[4]

The failure is information—vital data that helps Jenneke run her best. As an avowed perfectionist myself, I need all the self-awareness I can muster to view failure so philosophically. But when I do, life as a whole flows with much more grace— even if the fall hurts sometimes.

*   *   *

In the late 1950s, a British industrialist proposed a contest, inviting folks to build an airplane powered entirely by human effort. After almost twenty years of complicated and failed solutions, a man named Paul MacCready pulled it off, building what would come to be known as the Gossamer Condor and the Gossamer Albatross. How did he do it? According to Aza Raskin, he knew the other inventors were solving the wrong problem:

> Paul realized that what needed to be solved was not, in fact, human-powered flight. That was a red herring. The problem was the process itself, and along with it the blind pursuit of a goal without a deeper understanding of how to tackle deeply difficult challenges. He came up with a new problem that he set out to solve: how can you build a plane that could be rebuilt in hours, not months. And he did. He built a plane with Mylar, aluminum tubing, and wire.
>
> The first airplane didn't work. It was too flimsy. But, because the problem he set out to solve was creating a plane he could fix in hours, he was able to quickly iterate. Sometimes he would fly three or four different planes in a single day. The rebuild, retest, relearn cycle went from months and years to hours and days.[5]

We are now heirs of Paul MacCready, living in a cultural moment that is learning to acknowledge failure, even frequent failure, as a wise teacher.

Failure:Lab, founded by Jordan O'Neil and Jonathan Williams, is an initiative in which successful people stand in front of a live audience and tell stories about their own failures: bankrupt businesses, broken relationships, personal crashes and burns. The point is to be a living testimony to the truths that failure happens, we can survive it, and we can learn from it.

After each Failure:Lab story, the audience sits in silence and considers what they've heard, sometimes tweeting their reactions as they relate the story to their own lives. Then an entertainer, often a musician, comes onstage to perform for a few moments to clear the air and prepare the space for the next story.

Many people wonder whether such a gathering would be depressing. On the contrary—attendees find them cathartic. For one thing, truth-telling and authenticity are always inspiring. They're what we secretly crave, even if we refuse to admit it. For another thing, the stories help drive home the fact that we all fail. Every one of us. The point is to find a way out (Exodus) in the wake of these failures. I recently ran across a long-forgotten bookmark, tucked in a book I'd started reading and later abandoned (a small failure in itself—ah, well). It said, "Show me the person who never makes a mistake and I'll show you the person who never makes anything."

Failure:Lab stories also remind us how much of life is outside our control. Sometimes failure happens through no fault of our own. The supplier we're counting on goes out of business. The financial person we hired robs us. The person we marry turns out to be completely different than we thought. Hindsight is often judgmentally 20/20 on these twists in circumstance, but the fact is, most of us are doing the best we can, and success and failure aren't entirely up to us.

"I have prayed for years for one good humiliation a day," writes author and priest Richard Rohr. "And then, I must watch my reaction to it."[6] It's the best way of recognizing where our ego has run amok, where we're holding on to our lives too tightly. Rohr is a spiritual giant, and I am not. The idea of praying for humiliation gives my perfectionistic heart uncomfortable palpitations. Besides, I have plenty of boneheadedness without asking God to give me more. But bit by little bit—one Miles-Davis-Thing-That-Happened at a time—I'm learning. And as Maya Angelou liked to say, "When you know better, you do better."[7]

Chapter 23

Embrace Ambiguity

May God bless you with discomfort
with easy answers, half truths, and superficial relationships,
so that you will live deeply
and from the heart.

Eugenia Gamble is a pastor who often uses these words as
a blessing to close conferences and worship services. After I
first heard these words, I added them to my own bag of tricks.
When I repeat them, I love watching people's reactions. The
word "discomfort" is the first sign that something's up; I can
usually see some double-takes and widened eyes. I understand, because that's how I reacted the first time I heard it.
They're expecting—just as I did—something predictable and
rather bland. May God bless us with compassion. Joy. Peace.
The biggies.

But this life of improvisation, this life of faith, isn't comfortable or predictable. If it is, we're doing it wrong. If we get
too comfortable, we better hope someone will say something
that makes our eyes snap open, so we can realize that we were
asleep and didn't know it.

After the four lines above, the blessing continues:

And may God bless you with anger
at injustice, oppression, and the exploitation of people,
so that you will work
for justice, freedom, and peace.

And may God bless you with tears to shed
for those who mourn,
so you will reach out your hand to them
and turn mourning into joy.

And may God bless you with just enough foolishness
to believe that you can make a difference in this world,
so that you will do those things that others say
cannot be done.[1]

Earlier we looked at the serenity prayer as an improviser's prayer. Here I want to introduce Eugenia Gamble's benediction as the improviser's blessing.

We need discomfort: What shakes us out of our complacency?
We need anger: What grabs us by the scruff of the neck and
    won't let us go until we respond?
We need tears: What breaks our hearts?
And we need foolishness: Foolishness is everywhere in life
    and in improv. But it's more foolish to believe that we
    can make a plan and stick to it 100 percent. It's foolish to
    believe that we're in control of our lives.

Discomfort, anger, tears, foolishness. These are the gifts of God for the people of God. These are the tools God bestows upon us so we can improvise, so we can look beyond the way things are to the way things ought to be—so we can live well even in the midst of uncertainty.

✳   ✳   ✳

Toward the end of one of my classes at the Training Center at Second City, we played a pattern game in which we joined in a circle and then yelled words across it in a specific order, "passing them" to one another again and again, faster and faster. We'd played the same game earlier in the week and had crashed and burned—but that day, late in the week, we were nailing every pattern. We were learning to perform together.

Our teacher layered a new set of words in a different pattern on top of the first, then another. (Think of it as juggling an increasing number of balls or spinning plates.) At first, we laughed with delight at each new challenge. But as she continued to add more and more patterns, our laughter became tinged with desperation. Some of us started to get downright angry. Others hunkered down in a kind of manic perfectionism, determined not to let any of the "spinning plates" fall to the floor.

I was one of those perfectionists: I *will control this. I will get it right.*

BUZZ. Nope.

Our teacher, a self-described "chaos monster," admitted that she'd set a failure trap for us. There was actually no way to win the game. The point was to see what happened when we were faced with an impossible task.

A friend who's better versed in *Star Trek* than I am later told me, "Oh, she put you through the Kobayashi Maru." This was the simulation used in Starfleet that put cadets into an unwinnable situation, with no possible escape for captain or crew. The simulation was designed to assess the cadets' character and grace under pressure. Captain Kirk was the only cadet to have beaten the Kobayashi Maru, but he did so by re-programming the simulation to allow for a positive out-come—because he didn't believe in no-win scenarios.

I wonder what Kirk would have done in our improv class.

How do we live with ambiguity? Do we double down, determined to stay on top of the chaos? (Guilty.) Or do we give up and walk away, muttering "This is stupid"? Or do we react as good improvisers do, holding ourselves lightly enough to know that we're not in control, and also able to celebrate our small successes and fleeting joys?

Even in my uber-focused scowling, I experienced moments of being held up by the energy of the group, and I didn't care about getting the pattern right. At other times I felt my senses heightened, and I was able to play the game with great precision. Those moments reminded me of *Star Wars* (my preferred sci-fi universe) and Obi-Wan Kenobi's description of the Force: the Force obeys our commands, but it can also control our actions.

So it is with life: we are called upon to be utterly pres-ent, participating to the best of our ability, while allowing ourselves to be carried along. Improv occurs amid these two paradoxes, working together.

✳   ✳   ✳

In 2014, best-selling author Daniel Pink delivered a provoca-tive commencement address to Northwestern University's Weinberg College of Arts and Sciences. "Sometimes," he said, "the only way to discover who you are or what life you should lead is to do less planning and more living—to burst the double bubble of comfort and convention and just do stuff, even if you don't know precisely where it's going to lead, because you don't know precisely where it's going to lead."

"This might sound risky," Pink continued. "And you know what? It is. It's really risky. But the greater risk is to choose false certainty over genuine ambiguity."[2]

During my time as a pastor, I had the opportunity to get to know a family who was dealing with a medical crisis. This crisis required them to seek treatment for their son at a children's hospital in Minnesota. I visited them a couple of times while they were there—once when it was close to the end of the boy's life, when the options were starting to narrow and it was looking more and more like he wouldn't survive.

After spending the day with the family at the hospital, I checked into a nearby hotel to get some sleep before flying out the next morning. I was engaging in some small talk with the desk clerk when she asked what brought me to Minneapolis. In very general terms I told her about the crisis.

She was shocked. "He's very sick, huh? ... So, is he going to be OK?" she asked, her eyes wide with concern.

"Well ... it really doesn't look good, unfortunately."

She was persistent. "But he's going to get better, isn't he?"

I looked at her a moment and then said, "Yes. Yes, he's going to be fine."

Her shoulders relaxed. And she had every bit of empathy and compassion you could imagine for this little boy she had no connection to, aside from helping his tired pastor find a place to stay. But ultimately she didn't have any space in her mind, her workday, her routine to absorb the fact that this little boy probably wasn't going to make it, and there was nothing anyone could do about it, and it made no sense.

She knew from my body language that I was lying to her. But I told her what she wanted to hear, enough so she could make it through her shift. I gave her some false certainty, I suppose.

In a way I can't blame her. I told her a convenient fiction that helped her get through the day. Because it's disturbing to live in a world in which the miracle doesn't happen.

* * *

I wish false certainty worked, but it has disappointed me time and again. As a person of faith, I want a God who's reliable, who's going to respond in ways I can predict. As far as I can tell, though, that kind of God doesn't exist. I'm not happy to be left with a God who works within genuine ambiguity. But ultimately, it's what we have.

We all share in those lies of convenient fiction from time to time, telling ourselves that everything will be OK. And false certainty is all around us. Marketing deceives us into believing that we can cheat death with the right smoothie blender. Books tout ten steps to a happy marriage. Removing our shoes before boarding a plane offers us a sense of security. But "certainty comes at the price of both liberty and creativity," writes Benedictine nun and author Joan Chittister. "It nails our feet to the floor and calls it a success."[3] False certainty keeps us stuck.

Earlier we talked about Job, who had everything taken away from him and whose friends insisted that his suffering must have been his fault. After some thirty chapters of railing against and pleading with God for an explanation, for *something*, Job finally gets a response. God addresses Job with a bombastic reminder that it was God, not Job, who was there at the foundation of the world, creating the universe, hemming in the chaos, guiding all that is.

In all the tumult of the whirlwind that began right before God spoke, it's easy to miss the fact that God *doesn't answer Job's question*. There is no divinely illuminated reason for Job's suffering. What Job receives instead is God's wild and unmistakable *there-ness*.

Curiously, Job seems satisfied by the encounter. Perhaps this is because, as much as we're drawn to the cheap allure of false certainty, genuine ambiguity is a much more resourceful companion. She's gruff and no-nonsense. She never sugarcoats things. When we ask "But why?," she snorts and says, "What does it even matter?"

She's with us and for us for the long, tough haul, never leaving our side. She's short on explanations but long on presence. And that presence turns out to be enough.

Principle 7

Go Off-Plan

The real difference between God and human beings, he thought, was that God cannot stand continuance. No sooner has he created a season of a year, or a time of the day, than he wishes for something quite different, and sweeps it all away. No sooner was one a young man, and happy at that, than the nature of things would rush one into marriage, martyr-dom, or old age. And human beings cleave to the existing state of things. All their lives they are striving to hold the moment fast.... It is all wrong, he thought, to imagine paradise as a never-changing state of bliss. It will probably, on the contrary, turn out to be, in the true spirit of God, an incessant up and down, a whirlpool of change. Only you may yourself, by that time, have become one with God, and have taken to liking it.

— Isak Dinesen, "The Monkey"[1]

We've spent the last six sections talking about ways to approach life as improv. We've also considered the ways in which God works improvisationally. Still, many of us approach this work while continuing to cling to the idea that God has a grand road map but chooses not to reveal it to us. There is a master plan; it's just not ours to know.

But what if that's not true?
What if there is no master plan?

Chapter 24

Meet the Mystery

In the last section, I shared a story of a very sick boy I visited in the hospital. I'd like to share that story in fuller detail here. It's a hard story to tell, but it's important. When people ask me where my interest in improvisation comes from, I tell them that it grew out of a time when my faith was shaken to the core.

When I first met the Osman family as the brand-new pastor of their church, their eight-year-old son Eric was gravely ill. He'd recently been diagnosed with adrenoleukodystrophy (ALD), a metabolic disease that affects the brain and nervous system. His mother had taken him to a children's hospital in Minneapolis to receive a bone marrow transplant. It was a Hail Mary effort, given how weakened he already was. Unfortunately, the transplant didn't reverse or halt this terrible disease, and Eric died the day before his ninth birthday.

The community grieved, and we struggled to comprehend the incomprehensible.

Meanwhile, the doctors began closely monitoring Jacob, Eric's younger brother. Jacob also had the genetic markers for ALD, but was asymptomatic so far. He started receiving an MRI every six months to make sure his brain remained normal. We prayed before every appointment. We rejoiced at every normal result.

Until the results weren't normal. Until Jacob's scan showed early signs of ALD progression.

Time was of the essence, so the family and medical team sprang into action. Recognizing that an early bone-marrow transplant might save Jacob, they rushed him to the same Minneapolis hospital where Eric had been treated. The parallels were chilling, except this time we were catching the disease early, while Jacob was otherwise a strong, healthy boy—strong enough, we hoped, for the treatment to be successful.

*   *   *

As human beings we're compelled to create stories and find connections—to make meaning of the events of our lives. We can't help ourselves. It's why we see coincidences and assign great significance to them, giving little thought to the thousands of things that happen to us that *aren't* coincidental.

The family and the congregation were devastated and frightened when the ALD began to show its hulking ugliness in Jacob's life. But even in the midst of the fear, people at the church (and elsewhere, I suspect) started building a narrative for this experience. I saw it happen in tiny ways: in snatches of conversation over coffee, after the church choir rehearsal, and while making sandwiches for the homeless ministry. I participated in these conversations myself. It's what people often want from their pastor—assistance in articulating the stories that help shape our lives.

The narrative went something like this:

Eric's death was not OK. It could never be OK. But maybe, just maybe, something good could come from it. Maybe Jacob's life would be spared, because Eric's ordeal warned us to be vigilant for any sign of disease. Ultimately Eric could not be saved, but maybe he could save his little brother's life because Jacob's treatment would come in time. Maybe Eric could give his brother the gift of the future he was not able to experience himself.

It's not the story we would have written for this family—or anyone, for that matter—if we'd been given a blank sheet of paper. Any story we authored from scratch would never have featured ALD. But given what had happened, ours was a story with a bit of redemption and grace in it. It was a story of God bringing good out of terrible circumstances. It was a story with familiar touchstones in it. These are the kinds of narratives that inspire us. Life after death. Grace.

Jacob's bone marrow transplant was successful—it halted the ALD progression. The church community and other friends and family waited for each update from Minnesota and rejoiced when the "good numbers" ticked upwards. But then Jacob got sick. The transplant cells were knocking out the ALD, but they were also knocking *him* out in an affliction called graft-versus-host disease. Each day was a new battle—to manage symptoms, to build up his strength, to buy some time so the bone marrow cells could continue to do their work.

I spoke to the family often—to Jacob's mother, Leslie, by phone, and during a couple of fleeting visits to Minnesota; and to Jacob's father, Bob (still working and holding down the homefront in Virginia), at lunches and on Sunday mornings, before and after church. As their pastor, I was desperate to provide some spiritual sustenance for the family, but I felt just as helpless as everyone else. Like so many others, I'd written this script, you see. And I was wedded to it. Eric would save his brother. Life out of death. We expected—needed—the story to fit our pre-planned narrative, and this did not fit. Jacob was supposed to get better.

And then came the gradual slide into the unthinkable. The desperate last-ditch treatments. The final prayers at the bedside. And then, on a September afternoon, the second of two boys, also lost at the age of eight. And Rachel, their sister, gone from middle child to oldest child to only child in just three years.

As a pastor, I thought there was nothing harder than doing a memorial service for a child. But there is: doing a memorial service for a child with the constant memory of what we did last time.

*   *   *

The death of a child is excruciating, and it tests any ideas about God's providence. But in my view, the death of two children in one family completely vaporized any notion of God's unchanging and all-encompassing plan. Still, there were people who, in a genuinely tenderhearted attempt to be comforting, said things that made me cringe.

"God never gives us more than we can handle."
"Everything happens for a reason."
"God needed another angel in heaven."

Sometimes I felt like my main job as a pastor was to stand in the way of these comments and shield the family from them. Of course, it's each person's job, and right, to make meaning of their own lives. Had the Osmans expressed these sentiments, I wouldn't have had an issue. What put me in protective mode was other people trying to do that work for them—whether out of concern or a misguided attempt to manage their own discomfort in this terrible situation.

Some people truly find solace in the idea that a time will come when the curtain will be pulled back and we'll see how everything fit together, like some cosmic Rube Goldberg device. If I were ever to find out that this is how God works— that God sends misfortune upon us in order to test us, or for some other reason—I'd renounce my ordination and go sell running shoes, because God and I would be finished. As David Bentley Hart wrote following the 2004 tsunami which took the lives of some 230,000 people, "It seems a strange thing to find peace in a universe rendered morally intelligible at the cost of a God rendered morally loathsome."[1]

*   *   *

In trying to come to terms with what happened—forget "making sense" of it—I tried to find a home along the theological continuum. I wasn't ready to give up on God altogether, but neither did I resonate with a God who pulled the strings, made the plans, and had to fill a quota of little blond eight-year-old angels in heaven. "There is more undeserved suffering in the world than faith can contain," someone wrote to me recently, and I felt the power of those words as I chafed against the easy answers.

The middle ground felt comfortable enough—God grieves with us; God can bring good out of bad circumstances—and yet it seemed incomplete. I longed for more.

As I sought to find words to understand God's action in the midst of this family's pain, I kept coming back to the incredible medical personnel whom I saw caring for these two boys. Medical crises don't follow a schedule or a plan. Every day requires flexibility, new approaches, and improvisation. Yes-And.

Each morning in Minnesota, doctors, nurses, techs, and social workers huddled around the medical charts during rounds, scanning the previous day's events and setting a course for the day to come. They were improvising: *What did we try yesterday that worked or didn't work? What might healing look like for the patient today?* They were working together to answer a basic question: *Given what we have to work with, what is the best Yes-And possible?*

The work of serving Jacob changed day by day. At first, the Yes was to halt the ALD and save his life.

As circumstances changed, the Yes changed:

To keep his body strong while it fought the graft-versus-host disease.

To help him keep some food down.

To manage the pain.

To get him successfully through an infusion of mesenchymal stem cells, a last resort.

To keep him alive until his father could make the final journey from Virginia to say good-bye.

What didn't change was the medical personnel's commitment to see the situation as it was, to be adaptable, and to bring their best efforts to caring for him.

This revelation sent me to Scripture. And as I considered God's action in the sacred story—especially the God we encounter in Jesus, who took on human limitation for our

sake—I didn't see a God with a plan. I saw a God who improvises, like those dedicated hospital workers. I saw a God who is
creative and dynamic, working with us to bring about the best
wholeness—the best Yes—at any given moment.

∗   ∗   ∗

Many years ago, in response to the terrorist attacks on September 11, 2001, PBS's *Frontline* program produced a special
episode, "Faith and Doubt at Ground Zero." The program
lifted up many different people who offered their view of the
meaning of the tragedy. Several voices echoed a familiar but
achingly narrow line: "God had a purpose in this, and who am I
to question it? How can I know better than God what's right? I
just have to accept this as God's plan."

I'm not sure what it says about me that the person whose
response I resonated with most was an orthodox rabbi. He
talked about how often people come to him with questions
about the meaning of suffering. He said, "I think my job as
a rabbi is to help people live with those questions. If God's
ways are mysterious, then we have no choice but to live in the
mystery. It's upsetting, it's scary, it's painful, it's deep, and it's
interesting. But no plan. That's what mystery is."[2]

No plan. Just God. A love-oriented, collaborative, relational, improvising God.

∗   ∗   ∗

Principle 7 of an improvising life is about getting beyond
ideas of the grand plan. Maybe your theology is such that
you know God has a plan, and that assurance comforts and

sustains you. I admire your steadfastness. I even envy you a little. But maybe you, like me, are curious about other ways to understand God's action in the world. If so, read on, and we'll discover together where the preceding six principles have been inevitably leading.

Chapter 25

Crack the Code

What should I do with my life?
How should I choose a major? A life partner? A place to live?
Should I have children? Move to Bangkok?
Train for an Ironman?

We may relate to improv as a tool for small-scale decisions and actions. But how does improv guide us in big decisions that may impact our lives for a long time to come? How do we learn to have a spirit of improvisation with circumstances that don't turn on a dime, that come to fruition slowly?

For those who believe that God has a plan for each of our lives, the task becomes focused on figuring out what that plan is. Discernment is a matter of testing out the many possible options and finding the one that's right.

Improv approaches things differently. If God is an improvising God—without a master plan, improvising with us—then our task becomes simultaneously harder and easier.

It's harder because we have to sift through many possible options for our life—any of which could be a fruitful path.

And it's easier because we're freed from the anxiety over getting it wrong. Any situation in which we find ourselves is an opportunity to Yes-And. God's loving nature is unchanging, focusing on the best Yes, the deepest wholeness. But God's actions are multivalent; there may be many possible paths to accomplish God's ends.

My husband, Robert, has had a fulfilling career in IT and computer security, doing a number of different things over his twenty-plus years in that field. Not all of his jobs have been awesome. Yet he's satisfied with the path he's taken. And aside from a brief stint with a career counselor as he contemplated some big shifts, he doesn't put that much thought into The Next Step or how a specific move will "set him up" for the move after that. There's no five- or ten-year plan. He's simply done the next right thing as it's presented itself.

The whole thing drives me a little batty because I am by nature a goal-setter and plan-maker. It feels reactive to do it his way. But I can't argue with what I see, which is a man who's content with where he is, and who somehow ends up with satisfying work that puts food on the table. It sounds like the Yes-And of improv, doesn't it?

Certainly there are times when we need to have an eye toward the future. If we sense a call towards a career that involves specialized training, for example, we aren't going to tumble our way into a graduate school or vocational program. But even when the path forward involves a series of hoops, we can still approach those moments with the soul of an improviser—with eyes and hearts open, ready to adjust course and embrace the unexpected.

What Robert illustrates is what David Brooks describes in a 2010 *New York Times* column as the "summoned self." "Life isn't a project to be completed; it's a landscape to be explored," he wrote. We must be able to respond to life situations as they come, asking, "What is this situation summoning me to do?"[1]

This approach, too, is improv: it's a responsiveness, a willingness to embrace a call when it comes, to receive a gift when it is offered. It's not a decision made once, but a lifelong journey of responding to God's call, God's summons.

*   *   *

When I was studying to be a pastor and pursuing ordination, I drew inspiration from a quote from writer and theologian Frederick Buechner: "The place God calls you to is the place where your deep gladness and the world's deep hunger meet."[2]

These words were practically tattooed on people's foreheads as we bustled our way toward paid ministry in the church. Now that I've been out of seminary for a while, I have a different perspective. I know many people whose work is nowhere near that sweet spot of personal satisfaction and societal need. Their "true calling" feels beyond their reach. I can see how they would feel like their gladness and the world's need never intersect, but instead run parallel to each other.

The problem I see is that Buechner is writing about the intersection of two lines at a single point—and a single point is too static for an improvised life, in which many of us will have multiple *careers*, let alone multiple jobs. And even if we agree that the "Buechner point" changes over time, it suggests that we should constantly look for one right answer, which always seems elusive.

In recent years, the words of Howard Thurman have invited me into a different view of calling: "Don't ask what the world needs. Ask yourself what makes you come alive and go do that. Because what the world needs is people who have come alive."[3]

Thurman's words seem appropriate for an improvised life. In improv there's a guiding principle to "follow the fun." We aren't obligated to pursue every Yes-And that comes along, especially the ones that don't seem to have any energy. We're on the lookout for the scene or character or idea that gives us joy, and then we pursue that to see where it takes us.

Some of the friends with whom I went to seminary have, over time, moved into positions at larger and larger churches. If there's a ministry career "ladder," they're climbing it faithfully and fruitfully. Others have formed their own faith communities and are pursuing ministry with no road map whatsoever. Still others are strong activists, deeply engaged in their communities, agitating for change.

As for me, I write. I tell stories of these big churches and nascent little communities. And I lead retreats and conferences to help people live authentic, improvisational lives.

Every job has its downsides, and mine is no exception. I travel a lot of weekends, which takes its toll on our family. Author/speaker doesn't bring in a lot of money (and I'm privileged that our household doesn't rely solely on my income). But much of the time, my work is so gratifying that it feels like cheating. *It should be harder than this*, The Voice chides. *You must not be doing anything important if it's this easy.*

Then I remember the improv dictum to do what's obvious. Given my circumstances and my set of gifts, of course this is what I would do at this stage of my life. Parish ministry may call me back in the future, and if it does, it will be because it offers me a chance to come alive within a particular community once again, in all of its joys, sorrows, triumphs, and challenges.

✳   ✳   ✳

Thurman's invitation to do what makes us come alive offers good guidance for an improvised life. If there's any limitation to his advice, it's the command to "go and do." Sometimes, we don't have the option to "go." Sometimes, for various reasons, we're called upon to stay put. Our child needs the premium health insurance that the uninspiring job provides. One spouse has a career that's geographically limiting, so the other spouse must make do. What then?

When our kids were younger, we used to watch the show *Dirty Jobs*. The host, Mike Rowe, would tag along as blue-collar workers demonstrated the various "dirty jobs" they pursued for a living. Rowe would make game attempts to learn at the feet of lamb castraters and spider-venom collectors, and his humor and respect for the people he met made the show fun and watchable.

Several years ago Rowe wrote a piece for *Forbes* about the advice many adults give young people to "follow their passion" into the right career for them:

> In the long history of inspirational pabulum, "follow your passion" has got to be the worst.... Over and over, people love to talk about the passion that guided them to happiness. When I left high school—confused and unsure of everything—my guidance counselor assured me that it would all work out, if I could just muster the courage to follow my dreams. My Scoutmaster said to trust my gut.

And my pastor advised me to listen to my heart. What a crock.

Why do we do this? Why do we tell our kids—and ourselves—that following some form of desire is the key to job satisfaction? If I've learned anything from [Dirty Jobs], it's the folly of looking for a job that completely satisfies a "true purpose."

In fact, the happiest people I've met over the last few years have not followed their passion at all—they have instead brought it with them.[4]

Mike Rowe is describing improv, a bloom-where-you're-planted mentality that sometimes means saying yes to being a sewer inspector or roadkill cleaner, even if that's not where we thought our "bliss" would take us. Yes, at times we can feel truly stuck in circumstances that kill our spirit and exhaust our energy. To the extent that we can change those circumstances, we should. (Remember the improviser's prayer in Chapter 2—to change the things we can and accept the things we can't.) At the same time, we do have a choice about how we respond—how we "And" our lives. As travel writer Rick Steves likes to say, "If something isn't to your liking, change your liking."[5]

*   *   *

Some time ago, I was with a group of improvisers, preparing for a show. After a few warmup games, while we waited for our turn onstage, our group's instructor asked, "So tell me what you appreciated about your performance in the showcase." We all paused for a moment—our instructor's first language was Spanish, and I wondered briefly if we'd misunderstood.

But no, he meant exactly what he said: he was asking us to talk about the show *as if it had already happened.*

So we did.

I liked that we got to the who-what-where of the scene really quickly.
I appreciated that there wasn't any dead space during the show.
I loved the way we all had each other's backs.

This was a revelation. By making these statements, we set our intentions for the experience we were about to have. And we spoke our reality into existence. We did find the who-what-where. We did fill the silence with ideas. We did have each other's backs.

The churchy analogy here is what's known as eschatology—the branch of theology that thinks about the fulfillment of promises made in Scripture. Most Christians I hang out with don't like to talk about eschatology because it can get into some nuttiness over the end times and an antichrist and other fantastical stuff. I try to hold the topic lightly by asking questions like these: "Where are we headed? If God is love, what are God's ultimate hopes for this creation? How are those hopes already in evidence? How are they not yet realized?"

Many of us have been part of an experience or project that kicked off with other questions: "What do we all hope to get out of this? What are our goals?" Those questions are fine, as far as they go. But by asking us to speak about the showcase as if it were completed, our instructor asked us to place ourselves in the future already—to sense what that accomplishment would feel like in our bodies, to picture ourselves at our best, and to experience the fulfillment of our hard work.

I'd like to try this with a group of people sometime—to have them think about their whole lives this way. To speak about their future as if it has already happened. I suspect that, were we to do so, we wouldn't have a list of specific career achievements. We'd say things that revealed general themes and values.

I never stopped learning.
I was loved by many, but ticked off a few as well.
I sought to live fearlessly.

So ... *should* you have children? Move to Bangkok? Train for an Ironman?

Very few questions like these have one definitive right answer. And if we're living improvised lives, we realize that "should" rarely appears. Instead, like David Brooks, we explore the landscape; like Mike Rowe, we take our passion with us into whatever we end up doing. And we never arrive. But, over time, we hope to become more fully ourselves, in ways that are somehow surprising and yet familiar at the same time.

Chapter 26

Fight Back with Beauty

Do not be daunted by the enormity of the world's grief. Do justly, now. Love mercy, now. Walk humbly, now. You are not obligated to complete the work, but neither are you free to abandon it.
　　　　　　　　　　　　　　　　　　　　—Rabbi Tarfon[1]

I stand by every word of this book. I'm convinced that Yes-And is the way forward. We've got to have our eyes and our hearts wide open, even when it hurts. Then we take the next faithful step, however small or obvious it might be. And, bit by bit, we make the path by walking the path.

And still, the world does what the world does.

As I write this chapter, fifty people are dead in Orlando, Florida, gunned down at a gay nightclub on Latin night during Pride month.

By the time you read this, the world will have moved on to something else. But right now, for me, writing to you from the past, this is the biggest mass shooting in our country's history. With some bizarre luck, that disgraceful record will still be standing. But right now the hurt is planet-sized. Investigators in the club are examining the crime scene while cell phones ring, over and over, as people frantically seek word about their loved ones.

Some parents will find out their child is gay at the same time they find out he or she is dead.

Yes does not come easy today. I'm tired of doing it, and I resent being asked to do it under these gruesome circumstances.

Life is constantly handing us stuff. Gifts, sometimes. Tragedies, too often. Opportunities, all the time. To be the change we wish to see in the world. To respond to hate with love. To not let the darkness have the last word.

But the darkness feels unyielding. And I'm exhausted. Where is the hope? Where is the grace? It's always our call to be on the lookout for it, but that detective work gets really tiresome.

Today it doesn't seem as if the Yes is winning. It doesn't feel as if things are getting better. Instead, we're barely holding the darkness at bay.

People line up to give blood, join hands, give money, write letters to Congress. We follow Mr. Rogers's advice to "look for the helpers" in times of crisis and tragedy.

We fumble our way to Yes.

But the Yes seems so small. I'm stuck with King Theoden from *Lord of the Rings*, on the ramparts of Helm's Deep, watching with mounting disgust and despair as an invading army wreaks destruction. He turns to Aragorn and says in a flat voice, "So much death. What can [we] do against such reckless hate?"[2]

What can we do against the worst mass shooting in our nation's history? What can we do against the unrelenting power of chaos, of decency and dignity coming ever unspooled?

Imagine what we could accomplish if we didn't have to Yes amid such horror. If we could pile Yes upon life-giving Yes and actually make progress, rather than expend our energy simply to keep from sliding into chaos.

*　　　*　　　*

In Suzanne Collins's dystopian novel *The Hunger Games*, a group of young people are chosen to fight to the death against their fellow "tributes," in a specially designed arena, for the entertainment of the decadent and corrupt Capitol. The Games are a means of social control, keeping the surrounding districts cowed by requiring them to sacrifice their sons and daughters in this grotesque yearly ritual.

In her struggle to survive in the arena, protagonist Katniss Everdeen befriends a young tribute named Rue. Rue isn't tough or strong—an alliance with her isn't a tremendous asset to Katniss. But Rue is clever and her heart is true, and she and Katniss manage to gain a couple of advantages over the others. But then, sadly, Rue is killed.

And something breaks open in Katniss.

The Hunger Games is a reality show. Everything the tributes do in the arena is broadcast for the entire country to see. Katniss knows that a hovercraft will be along soon to pick up Rue's body and remove it from the arena. She feels moved to do something to acknowledge her friend, but she knows she doesn't have much time. She must show the Capitol that there's a part of her that they cannot control. And so she gathers white flowers from a nearby meadow and places them around Rue's head, in her arms, around her body. She does this in memory of her friend, in recognition of her worth—not as a pawn in the Capitol's power games, but as a human being. Katniss does this so everyone will see and know: Every human being has a dignity that can never be taken away.[3]

As it happens, Katniss's small Yes sets things in motion for a revolution that will unfold over two more books, as a nation of oppressed people find the hope and courage to fight back against the indulgent and oppressive Capitol.

But at this moment, as I sit devastated over Orlando, here's what strikes me about Katniss's honoring of Rue. It's wonderful when our small acts of Yes create ripples beyond what we ever imagined. It makes for great stories. And it can change things in ways we couldn't have foreseen.

But the ripples don't always happen.

Honoring Rue was the right thing for Katniss to do, even if no revolution followed—even if nobody saw it happen, in fact—because Yes is always worth saying. It saves one's own life, even if no other life can be saved.

✳   ✳   ✳

In the days following 9/11, writer Sally Schneider and her boyfriend found themselves wandering the deserted and devastated streets of New York and finding a restaurant open. It was an Italian restaurant. The owner, standing at the door, said, "Yes, we're open," and welcomed them in. There was something so comforting about the food people shared in that place—as if life were normal somehow.

It almost felt defiant.... I would compare it to Katniss decorating the body of an "expendable" tribute with flowers.

Later, Sally described the experience to a friend—*What was it about that meal that made it so significant?*—and her friend said, "We fight back with beauty."[4]

Since then, "fight back with beauty" has become one of my touchstones, in the wake of Orlando and so many events like it, when I'm faced with systemic injustice and planetary peril. We fight back with beauty—and Yes is an expression of beauty.

We don't say Yes because it will move the cause of justice and peace forward, though we hope it does. We don't improvise because it's the most effective way to live, though it might be. We do it because that's all there is. There is no other option. The alternative is passive oblivion.

I'm told that St. Benedict, in his rules for monasteries, put in a quirky little provision for new novices—new members of the community. He wrote that every newcomer who was ready to take his vows would surrender his street clothes and receive the clothing of the monastery ... but his street clothes would remain in an unlocked closet, next to the traditional Benedictine attire. In this way, the novice would have to make a choice each day to live in the spirit of the community. Will I *choose this way of life again? Will I put on the identity of the monk once again? Will I say Yes?*[5]

Well ...
what will we choose?

Bringing Improv to Life:
Exercises for Individuals and Groups

The exercises here, provided chapter by chapter, can be used to deepen the "reading experience" of this book. The "Try It" exercises are more reflective in nature; both individuals and groups can benefit from working through them. The "Play To-gether" activities are simple improv games that even beginner groups can do to engage more meaningfully with the book. All you need for these activities is a group with a willing spirit and an atmosphere of trust. (Interestingly, these exercises help create that spirit and that trust. You're building the bridge as you walk on it.)

Feel free to adjust the activities based on the needs of your group (e.g., people with limited mobility can do many of the games seated). If the instructions aren't clear to you and you're unsure how to proceed, make a choice and go for it. Fun and exploration are the goals, not perfection. If you can, end the play while the energy is still high.

Each of the group exercises here has been chosen to com-plement a specific chapter. Some connections may be obvious; others may be more indirect. But that's the nature of improv—it doesn't follow a linear path or lead to a pre-set outcome. It may be helpful to debrief after every exercise with questions like these: "What about this exercise was hard for you? What was easy? What did you notice about how the group worked together?" One of my teachers likes to debrief with a simple "Tell me about it." Don't worry if the resulting conversation doesn't relate to the chapter topic. Trust the process.

PRINCIPLE I: SAY YES

Chapter 1: Live Yes-ly

Try It
Do a "Yes" audit of your life. Take a day and pay attention to every time you say "Yes" and every time you say "No." Don't try to change anything at this point; just notice. Are there certain situations or people who elicit one or the other? What's that about?

Play Together: "That's Awesome!"
Have the group form itself into a loose circle, sitting or standing. Then go around the circle, having each person say something that's true about themselves. It can be absolutely anything—cleverness isn't required. "I have brown shoes." "I had a flat tire on the way here." In response, everyone else pumps their arms into the air and exclaims "That's awesome!" in unison. The game helps people get to know each other and reinforces saying "Yes" to other people's offers.

Chapter 2: Accept What We Can't Change

Try It

Make the serenity prayer—I mean the *improviser's* prayer—a regular part of your day, in whatever way works for you. Post it somewhere you'll see it regularly. Say it to yourself each morning or evening, or during your commute, or when a loved one is trying your nerves. Write it out in a journal or on a white board each day. Live with it for a week and see what happens.

Play Together: "Die! Not Today!" (with optional puppies)

Have the group form itself into a loose circle. One person starts by looking at someone across the circle, throwing an imaginary knife, and saying "Die!" The recipient catches the knife unharmed and says "Not today!" Then the recipient passes the knife to someone else in the same way. Have the group continue until each person has received and thrown a couple of times.

Optional next step: Keep the knife going around the circle, but start a separate motion of someone lobbing an imaginary basket of puppies while saying "Basket of puppies!" Now everyone's job is to pass the knife while also protecting the puppies. This helps people pay attention and cooperate. It also gets people laughing. (And I haven't lost a human or a canine yet.)

Note: Some groups find the "violent" subtext of this game disturbing; others find "Not today!" an affirmative statement of survival and defiance. You know your people. Feel free to substitute other words and motions to pass around the circle. Use your imagination.

Chapter 3: Listen for God's Yes

Try It

How does "Everything happens for a reason" strike your ears, mind, and heart? In what ways does it make sense to you? In what ways do you recoil from it? Take a page from Exodus, "a way out." Look back on a moment in your life when everything seemed to come together. Brainstorm all the other wonderful ways it could have turned out too. Have fun with it!

Play Together: Zen Count

Have the group gather in a tight circle, either with eyes closed or with people looking down, not making eye contact. The object of the game is to count from one to twenty-one, one voice at a time. Simple? The catch: any time two people speak at the same time, the group starts over with one. This game encourages slowing down and engaging a different kind of listening. I can't explain how it works, but it does. Continue past twenty-one if you wish. I was in a group once that got past ninety. Remarkable!

Chapter 4: Say No to Say Yes

Try It

A friend recently shared the story of her divorce. She told me that even though her marriage was ending and it was painful, she always thought of it as a Yes—Yes to a more happy and abundant life in the long run. Think about a difficult experience you've had. How would you reframe it as a Yes? You don't have to find that Yes convincing. Just give it a try, and give yourself grace to react to it in any way.

Play Together: Yes, Move
Have the group gather in a circle. One person begins by looking at another person in the circle and saying his or her name. The second person says "Yes," which gives the first person permission to begin walking to Person #2's spot. Person #2 must now ask another person for permission to move, and wait for a "Yes" before heading for the new spot. And so it goes. This exercise reinforces giving and receiving permission.

Chapter 5: Risk Yes

Try It
Ask yourself a simple but hard question: What would you do if you knew you couldn't fail? Or more to the point: What do you feel called to do, even if you *may* fail?

Play Together: Yes-And Superhero
Gather the group into a circle and ask for a suggestion of an imaginary superhero. (Tax Man. Wonder Weaver. I once did this with a group of Presbyterian pastors who came up with Presby-Girl.) Go around the circle and have each person describe one thing about that superhero—their appearance, super powers, back story, etc. After each offered detail, the rest of the group pumps their fists and says "YES!" It's fun when responses build on each other, but you're still working on Yes, so there are no wrong answers here. Continue as long as the energy remains high.

Principle 2: Say And

Chapter 6: Live toward And

Try It
Consider the categories of blocking, accepting, and over-accepting (or embracing) in your own life. When have you found yourself in each category? Which reaction is your default? How would you like to see that default change?

Play Together: No, Yes-But, Yes-And
Divide your group into pairs. Ask one person in each pair to offer a suggestion for something the pair might do together. ("Let's have a picnic!") Person #2 in each pair must then say "No" and offer an alternate suggestion. ("No, let's go to a basketball game.") This continues back and forth until the leader calls time, about 60 seconds. In the second round, Person #2 in each pair begins by making an offer, and Person #1 in each pair responds with "Yes, but ..." followed by an objection of some kind. ("Let's go to the movies." "Yes, but there's nothing good playing.") Continue back and forth as before, 60 to 90 seconds. In the third round, Person #1 in each pair initiates again, and this time Person #2 in each pair responds with "Yes, and ...," followed by something that builds on the offer. ("Let's go to the zoo." "Yes, and we can feed the seals!") This exercise teaches the power of Yes-And. Take particular note of how the energy changes in the room during the three rounds. Which was hardest? Which was easiest?

Chapter 7: Listen for God's And

Try It

The God we meet through Jesus is a God who always has another surprise in store, another card to play. Write a poem about God's And. Write the phrase "New life is ...," then complete the sentence. Repeat until you think you've run out of ideas, then keep going for a few more. You may tap into thoughts you didn't know you had. Fine literature isn't the goal; self-expression and spiritual exploration are.

Play Together: Questions

Divide the group into pairs. Have each pair engage in a simple conversation, but tell them they can only speak to each other in questions. Continue play for 30 to 45 seconds, then debrief the experience. What was easy or hard about only asking questions? Sometimes questions can keep us going in circles, but other times questions can lead us to unexpected places.

Chapter 8: Use And to Create Possibilities

Try It

In Chapter 1 we did a Yes audit. Now we're on the lookout for But. Have a loved one, co-worker, or trusted friend help you listen for "Buts" when you talk—not just the word itself, but also resistance in general.

Play Together: Picket Signs

This is a word-association game in which four words will become a chant. Get the group into a circle. Have one person say a word, then have the next person say another word that comes to mind, and then have person #3 and person #4 follow suit. Then have the entire group repeat those four words together, as if chanting at a rally.

Example:

Person 1: "Dog."
Person 2: "Food."
Person 3: "Smelly."
Person 4: "Chair."

All chant quickly: "Dog! Food! Smelly! Chair! Dog! Food! Smelly! Chair!"

Continue with the next four people and a new set of words. Go around the circle until all have participated and/or the fun is done. This exercise encourages quick thinking without judgment (the words don't need to relate, and often they don't), and also saying Yes-And (the group members support each other by chanting enthusiastically, no matter what word or phrase comes up).

Chapter 9: Embrace the Vulnerability of And

Try It
When is the last time you left a "you-shaped hole in the wall"—when you pursued something with your whole heart, soul, mind, and strength? It may be a task, a job, or a relationship. What happened? What might you do differently today? Remember to be kind to yourself in this exercise. Even if you made mistakes, you gave it all you had!

Play Together: Hot Spot

This is an exercise in Yes-And, as well as supporting one another in vulnerable situations. Begin by gathering people into a circle. Then have one person jump into the center and start singing a song, any song. Have the rest of the group sing along—even if they don't know the words, tell them to fake it, and fake it with enthusiasm! The game is fun if people support the heck out of the person in the middle, and it fizzles if people hold back and try to be cool. (Remind your group that cool has no place in improv.)

Now ramp up the game. If the person in the center sings a word that makes someone think of a different song, that person jumps into the middle and takes over, and game play continues. (Note: If the original singer has been in the center too long and it seems like time for a "rescue," have someone else jump in, even if they don't have any idea of what to sing. "Happy Birthday" always works.)

Example: "How do you solve a problem like Maria ..." can become "Maria ... I just met a girl named Maria," can become "Girls just wanna have fun...." Or the songs may have no discernible relationship. That's OK too.

PRINCIPLE 3: TRAIN YOUR VISION

Chapter 10: Cultivate Vision

Try It

Strive to be a deeper listener. Avoid multitasking whenever possible, and give your attention to one thing at a time. Catch yourself when you're listening in order to respond rather than listening to understand.

Play Together: What Else Can This Be?
Gather people into a group. Pass around a household item and
invite people to pantomime an alternate use for it. Example: A
metal water bottle becomes a vase, or a rolling pin, or a ham-
mer. Continue with other items for as long as the group seems
to be having fun.

Chapter 11: Pay Attention

Try It
Are you more naturally oriented toward deep attention or
hyper attention? Attention can be developed, like a muscle.
Consider a spiritual practice to work your non-dominant attention. For example, work on hyper attention by taking a medita-
tive walk in your neighborhood to notice small things. Practice
deep attention through meditation or contemplative prayer.

Play Together: Walk in Sync
Have the group mill around the room without speaking, moving however they feel comfortable. Invite people, as they feel
inclined, to clap once—everyone else's job is to see the clap
starting and clap at the same time. Ideally, you shouldn't be
able to tell who initiated the action. This exercise requires clear
non-verbal communication (How might the person "forecast"
that the clap is coming, without talking?) as well as careful
attentiveness on the part of the group.

After people have gotten used to this action, continue
with the clap, but add a second option: people may freeze for a
few seconds. Then, after working with these two actions, add a
third: jumping once into the air.

Chapter 12: *See Defeats Differently*

Try It

According to Chapter 12, "Finding the Yes-And amid horrible circumstances is defiant and stubborn: *We're gonna make something redemptive out of this mess.*" When have you seen this happen? When have you experienced it yourself? Is there a situation you're dealing with right now that needs this kind of improvisational approach?

Play Together: What Could Be Better? What Could Be Worse?

Have the group form a circle and ask one person to offer a simple sentence. ("I found a penny on the sidewalk.") Then have everyone say aloud together, "What could be better?" Then the next person adds to the previous statement in some way that ideally heightens the story and makes it better. ("And it was a magical penny!") The group responds again with "What could be better?" and the heightening continues with the next person. Have people continue around the circle. If the story seems to get stuck, encourage them to try to make their statement relate to the previous one if they aren't already doing so. For example, "I spilled the coffee all over myself" might be followed by "And I was wearing my favorite shirt" rather than "Then it started raining."

Once you've gone around the circle a few times and the story seems complete, do the same thing with a new opening statement and the question "What could be worse?" (Example: "I had a cold." "What could be worse?" "There was no hot tea in the house.")

Debrief the exercise. Which felt easier to build on, the better or the worse?

Principle 4: Find Your Troupe

Chapter 13: Play Well with Others

Try It
Burst your bubbles. Cultivating a good troupe means surrounding yourself with people who will Yes-And with you, *but who don't think exactly the way you do*. Go to lunch with someone who sees things differently. Read a reputable news source that comes at things from another angle. (Remember: You are under no obligation to subject yourself to abuse or bigotry.)

Play Together: What Are You Doing?
Have one person come to the front of the room and begin pantomiming a simple, recognizable action (e.g., fishing, playing hopscotch). After a few moments, have another person come up and ask, "What are you doing?" Person #1 then names an action *other than the one they're doing*. (If they're baking a cake, they might say, "Doing my taxes.") Then Person #2 begins doing that action, and Person #1 is finished and sits down. Next Person #3 comes up and says, "What are you doing?"—and so on. Game play continues this way as long as the group is having fun. End on a high note.

Chapter 14: Be a Pirate, a Robot, or a Ninja

Try It

Divide a sheet of paper into three sections and label them "Pirate," "Robot," and "Ninja." Write down the name of everyone in your life you can think of and put each into the category that makes the most sense to you. Don't worry too much about how these people might categorize themselves—what matters is what they bring out in you. Also, don't stress about categorizing people perfectly—people are more complicated than any typology. When you're finished, review the lists. What do you notice about your cast of characters? Who's missing? Is one type more represented than the others? What does that say to you?

Play Together: Tree, Nut, Squirrel

Gather people into a loose circle. Have one person move into the middle and assume a pose like a tree (however they envision it) and say, "I am a tree." Then have another person come in as the nut (again, however they envision that pose) and say, "I am a nut." The third person follows suit with "I am a squirrel." The first person (the tree) decides which of the other two people stays and announces it ("Squirrel stays"). And only the squirrel stays—the other two move back out to the circle. Then the squirrel re-announces himself or herself ("I am a squirrel"), and two other people come in as two things that might go with "squirrel" (e.g., "I am a hole"; "I am a birdfeeder"). The squirrel then decides which person stays ("Birdfeeder stays"), and the other two return to the circle. Play continues as long as the fun does.

Chapter 15: Serve One Another

Try It

For one week, commit to doing one small thing for someone else each day. See if you can find a mix between anonymous and non-anonymous actions. Don't shrug off any thanks you receive—accept it graciously and move on.

Play Together: Mirroring Game

Divide the group into pairs and have them stand or sit opposite each other. Have one person in each pair initiate a series of motions that the other person mirrors as exactly as possible. There's no need to be fast or fancy—players should just enjoy the slow, easygoing process of moving together. Ideally, an observer wouldn't be able to tell which person is leading and which person is following.

PRINCIPLE 5: FIND THE RIGHT STRUCTURE

Chapter 16: Get Lean

Try It

Try this at the end of a "typical" day (whatever that means). Review the events of the day—writing in a journal or talking with a friend—and note every decision you had to make, large or small. Take note of which decisions involved a lot of psychic energy. Can any of these decisions be offloaded? How might you streamline some of your mental processes?

Play Together: Once upon a Time …
Use the prompts on page 103 at the beginning of the section about Principle 5. Give each person in the group a sheet of paper and have them arrange themselves in a circle. Ask them to write "Once upon a time," complete the sentence, and then pass the paper to their right. Each of them will receive a paper from the person on their left. Have everyone continue the story on the paper they receive by writing "And every day …" and filling in the rest of the sentence. Continue passing and writing sentences based on the prompts until the stories are finished. Then have the group read aloud and enjoy what they created together through teamwork and just the right amount of structure.

Chapter 17: Take One Small Step

Try It
Consider a large task or goal you've been putting off. How might you break it into smaller steps? Just for fun, see how small you can make the steps. (A step in a writing project might be "Write a sentence." An even smaller step would be "Pick up the pen.")

Play Together: Bacon-and-Eggs Storytelling
The object of this game is for the group to make up a story, one word at a time. Arrange the group in a circle. Have one person start a story with a single word: "One." The next person in the circle will say that word, and a word that logically (or illogically) follows: "One day." The next person will repeat the two words and add a third: "One day, Jeremy …" The next

person will repeat the three words and add a fourth: "One day, Jeremy visited ..."—and so on. Someone can finish a sentence whenever it seems natural to do so with the word "period," and then the next person will start a new sentence—but he or she must repeat the previous sentence in its entirety first.

The catch is that someone will mess up. In this game, it's not only expected—it's celebrated. When someone says a word out of order or forgets where they are, everyone starts saying "Bacon and eggs! Bacon and eggs!" and rearranges themselves (scrambling themselves) in the circle. Then the group starts over. Play continues as long as the fun does.

Chapter 18: Plan Right

Try It
Consider one of the quotes from this chapter: "Plans are nothing, but planning is everything." Can you think of a time when you made a plan that changed dramatically in practice? How did the *process* of planning help you, even if the plan went off course? What does it mean for you to "Trust your training" in your own life?

Play Together: Collaborative Drawing
Arrange participants in a circle and give everyone a sheet of paper. Invite people to draw one simple doodle on their sheet—it shouldn't resemble anything specific. Then each person passes the sheet to their right and receives the sheet from their left. Invite everyone to continue the doodle they received by making something out of it—it could be abstract or not.

You can stop when people are done—or continue to pass the sheets around for further embellishments.

Chapter 19: Make Peace with "Not Enough"

Try It
Pick one goal or area of focus in your life (work, family, physical health). What would it mean for you to "embrace the shake" in this area? Try it.

Play Together: Lightning Scenes
Have two to three people come to the front of the room. Give them a fairy tale or other well-known story and have them act it out. Give them about 60 seconds to bring the story to life. The group shouldn't confer ahead of time—they'll figure out who plays which character as they go along (and they may have to double-up on roles—that's part of the fun). Then have them act out the same story, but with only 30 seconds. Then 20 seconds, then 10, and finally 5. It's a fast-paced exercise in embracing scarcity!

PRINCIPLE 6: LIVE MORE DEEPLY

Chapter 20: Wrestle with The Voice

Try It
Pick one of the strategies in this chapter for dealing with The Voice (make friends with it, make sure you're doing the right job, play Beat the Clock). Give it a try for one week and see

whether you're able to break through The Voice's efforts to put up resistance to whatever it is you want to accomplish.

Play Together: Chicken, Dinosaur, Superman
One way to quiet The Voice is to take ourselves less seriously. Here's a silly game that helps get people out of self-critical mode. Have everyone in your group mill around the room, clucking like a chicken. Have them pair up with others at random for a quick game of Rock Paper Scissors. Those who win the game "graduate" to acting like dinosaurs. Those who don't win stay chickens. Keep them milling around and finding new partners to play the game with. Every dinosaur who wins Rock Paper Scissors becomes Superman; every dinosaur who loses goes back to being a chicken. Every Superman who loses goes back to being a dinosaur; every Superman who wins stays a superhero. Have people move around constantly and quickly to find new playmates. Part of the fun is how quickly someone's luck can change in this game.

Chapter 21: *Refuse to Hoard*

Try It
Generosity is a virtue, but it's also a practice and a choice. How might you practice radical generosity this week? What do you find yourself hoarding—your time, your energy, your ideas, your money? Set an intention every day to be generous, and revisit that intention every night. Remember, in improv we bring a brick, not a cathedral: even a series of small steps can move the scene forward.

Play Together: Heightening Emotion

Give the group a simple emotion and ask them to mill around the room embodying that emotion. On a scale of 1 to 10 in terms of intensity, have them start at 1 or 2. Like a symphony conductor, call out higher numbers and have them heighten the emotion in response. (They can speak or make noise, but they aren't necessarily interacting with each other.) Then bring the intensity back down with decreasing numbers. Repeat with a new emotion.

Alternatively, you can designate certain areas of the room as certain numbers, so people can visit different intensities as they feel comfortable doing so.

Chapter 22: Reframe Loss and Failure

Try It

Plan your own Failure:Lab, alone or with friends. Tell the stories of the ways you've screwed up and what you've learned. For best results, choose events on which you have some critical distance, in which the mistakes aren't quite so fresh.

Play Together: Peas in a Pod

Set up two chairs side by side, facing the rest of the group. Then have two people sit down, and ask one person to express an opinion of some kind: "Cheesecake is the best dessert." The other person's job is to agree and add: "I know! And the cheese gives it protein, so it's healthy." Then the first person agrees and adds even further: "We should find out if there's a National Cheesecake Day, and if there isn't, we should make one!" The partners continue to agree, and take this agreement

to whatever absurd levels they can. The leader ends the scene
when it seems finished.

Play a few rounds of this game. Then, if you dare, and
the circumstances make it possible, have people think about
someone they disagree with, or with whom they're having
some kind of conflict. Then have them pair off, using these
conflicted situations as fodder for Peas in a Pod. One person
in every pair talks like the "conflict person," and the other
responds, building on that comment, so every pair continues
heightening and amplifying this perspective. (Example: A
parent, acting as her teenage child, says, "My mother is such
a drag, she makes me turn off my phone during dinner." The
partner agrees and says, "That is the worst. Doesn't she understand that you have friends you want to connect with!?")

Keep it light and safe—this is not the venue to process
deep trauma, and people certainly shouldn't choose somebody
in the room as their "conflict person." But remember the value
of the exercise: putting yourself in someone else's shoes can
sometimes bring out their perspective in ways that may surprise and benefit you.

Chapter 23: Embrace Ambiguity

Try It

There's a quote from Gilda Radner emblazoned on a wall in
the Second City Training Center: "Life is about not knowing
what's going to happen next—delicious ambiguity." Reflect
on this statement. Do you agree or disagree, wholeheartedly or
somewhat?

Play Together: Petting a Cat, Swinging a Bat

Have your group spread out and arrange themselves so they can see each other easily. Have one person start a simple, repetitive motion and announce what it is: "I'm petting a cat." Then have everyone else mimic the motion, repeating the motion and the phrase over and over.

The motion can change in one of two ways:

1. Someone does the same motion, but changes the context by identifying the motion differently. So "I'm petting a cat" becomes "I'm smoothing down the bedspread." The group would then start repeating the new phrase and motion.
2. Someone changes the motion to something completely different, but their descriptive phrase must rhyme with the previous phrase. So "I'm petting a cat" becomes "I'm swinging a bat." The group mirrors the new motion and repeats the new phrase.

Continue for several rounds.

Advanced version: Once the group has gone through several rounds, see if they can work their way backwards through the motions and phrases, reconstructing each move and how it connected to the previous one. (Note: This is hard, but why not try it? There are no detentions or failing grades in improv.)

Principle 7: Go Off-Plan

Chapter 24: Meet the Mystery

Try It
Sit in silence with this chapter, and any stories it calls to mind from your own life, and don't try to resolve or synthesize them. Just feel what you feel about them.

Play Together: Soundscapes
If physically possible, have everyone lie on their backs in a circle on the floor, with their heads toward the center of the circle. (They could also sit in chairs in a tight circle, facing out.) Turn off the lights and give people a few minutes to breathe deeply and relax. Then invite them, as they feel inclined, to make a simple noise—a bloop, a ding, whatever they want— and repeat it as often as they want. People will be making their own sounds at their own pace, so that, together, they create a soundscape. Let the sounds continue for a while—they usually quiet down on their own. This is often a relaxing activity and a good closing exercise for a group meeting.

Chapter 25: Crack the Code

Try It
Write a poem called "Come Alive," in which the lines are things that make you come alive, both large and small. Write as fast as you can, and don't worry about "poetic form." If you wish, color-code the poem afterward, highlighting in one color

those lines that surprised you, and highlighting in another color those ideas that feel familiar.

Play Together: Improv Goo
This is a silent game, played in pairs. Each pair is given some "improv goo"—imaginary stuff that can be shaped and molded, enlarged or reduced. Person #1 in each pair will work with the goo and make something out of it. After interacting with it for a moment (which helps Person #2 of the pair know what it is), they pass the object to their partner, who then interacts with it in some way. (Example: if Person #1 creates a balloon and blows it up, Person #2 might bounce it up in the air a few times.) Then Person #2 shapes the goo into something new, plays with it, then passes it back to Person #1. Let the game continue as long as it's fun for the group. Remind the players not to worry if they can't tell what their partners created. Once they "get the goo," they can do whatever they want with it.

Chapter 26: *Fight Back with Beauty*

Try It ... Together
The world can be an ugly, confusing, chaotic place. It can also be infused with great hope and beauty. Be a detective for beauty, and a promiscuous perpetrator of it. Find co-creators and hold each other accountable to "fight back with beauty."

Notes

Notes to the Introduction

1. Tina Fey, *Bossypants* (New York: Reagan Arthur Books, 2011), p. 84.

2. Emma Allen, "How the Upright Citizens Brigade Improvised a Comedy Empire," *The New Yorker*, September 5, 2016, http://www.newyorker.com/magazine/2016/09/05/upright-citizens-brigades-comedy-empire. Accessed September 19, 2017.

Notes to Principle 1

1. *Roxanne*, directed by Fred Schepisi (1987; Sony Pictures Home Entertainment, 1998), DVD.

Notes to Chapter 2

1. Fred R. Shapiro, "Who Wrote the Serenity Prayer?" *Yale Alumni Magazine*, July/August 2008, http://archives.yalealumnimagazine.com/issues/2008_07/serenity.html. Accessed September 21, 2017.

2. Ashley Goff, "Foundations of Improv Class," https://www.godofthesparrow.com/blog/the-landscape-of-liturgy-foundations-of-improv-class. Accessed September 21, 2017.

3. T. J. Jagodowski, David Pasquesi, and Pam Victor, *Improvisation*

at the Speed of Life: The TJ and Dave Book (New York: Solo Roma, 2015), p. 61.

4. NOVA, "Invisible Universe Revealed," written and directed by Peter Yost (PBS, April 22, 2015).

5. "Anne Lamott: Falling Off the Tightrope," Beliefnet, http://www.beliefnet.com/faiths/christianity/2006/06/anne-lamott-falling-off-the-tightrope.aspx. Accessed September 21, 2017.

Notes to Chapter 3

1. Thanks to Anna Carter Florence of Columbia Theological Seminary for this insight.

Notes to Chapter 5

1. My thanks to colleague Chris Tuttle for sharing this story in a preaching group in 2016.

2. William Sloane Coffin, *The Collected Sermons of William Sloane Coffin*, volume 2 (Louisville: Westminster John Knox Press, 2008), p. 251.

3. "Stephen Colbert Commencement Address," Knox College, http://departments.knox.edu/newsarchive/newsevents/2006/x12547.html. Accessed September 21, 2017.

4. Emma Allen, "How the Upright Citizens Brigade Improvised a Comedy Empire," *The New Yorker*, September 5, 2016, http://www.newyorker.com/magazine/2016/09/05/upright-citizens-brigades-comedy-empire. Accessed September 21, 2017.

5. C. S. Lewis, quoted by Courtney Reissig, "To Love Is to Be Vulnerable," *The Gospel Coalition*, August 8, 2013, https://www.thegospelcoalition.org/article/to-love-is-to-be-vulnerable. Accessed September 21, 2017.

6. Nicolaus Mills, "When Ralph Ellison and Gordon Parks Took on Harlem," The Daily Beast, June 19, 2016, http://www.thedailybeast.com/articles/2016/06/19/when-ralph-ellison-and-gordon-parks-took-on-harlem.html. Accessed September 21, 2017.

7. Parker Palmer, "A Life Lived Whole," *Yes Magazine*, November 8, 2004, http://www.yesmagazine.org/issues/healing-resistance/a-life-lived-whole. Accessed September 21, 2017.

Notes to Principle 2

1. Rosamund Stone Zander and Benjamin Zander, *The Art of Possibility: Transforming Professional and Personal Life* (New York: Penguin Books, 2002), p. 119.

Notes to Chapter 6

1. Samuel Wells, *Improvisation: The Drama of Christian Ethics* (Grand Rapids: Brazos Press, 2004).

Notes to Chapter 7

1. *Glory to God: The Presbyterian Hymnal* (Louisville: Westminster John Knox Press, 2013), #157.

2. Martin B. Copenhaver, *Jesus Is the Question: The 307 Questions Jesus Asked and the 3 He Answered* (Nashville: Abingdon Press, 2014).

3. God famously destroys these cities later. But for now, thanks to Abraham's direct intervention, they're safe.

Notes to Chapter 8

1. Kevin Loria, "Something weird happens to your brain when you start improvising," *Business Insider*, April 9, 2015, http://www.businessinsider.com.au/what-creativity-looks-like-in-the-brain-2015-4. Accessed September 21, 2017.

2. "And Not But Meeting Ground Rule," Podcast, Manager Tools, April 1, 2012, https://www.manager-tools.com/2012/03/and-not-meeting-ground-rule. Accessed September 21, 2017.

3. Elizabeth Drescher, "Vandalism as Conversation Starter," Religion Dispatches, June 3, 2013, http://www.religiondispatches.org/archive/culture/7120/vandalismasconversation_starter. Accessed September 21, 2017.

Notes to Chapter 9

1. Johannes Haushofer, "CV of Failures," Princeton University website, accessed March 2, 2017, https://www.princeton.edu/~joha/JohannesHaushoferCVofFailures.pdf. Accessed September 21, 2017.

2. "The Mystery and Art of Living," Podcast Interview between Pico Iyer and Krista Tippett, On Being, May 5, 2016, https://www.onbeing.org/programs/krista-tippett-the-mystery-and-art-of-living/. Accessed September 21, 2017.

3. T. J. Jagodowski, David Pasquesi, and Pam Victor, Improvisation at the Speed of Life: The TJ and Dave Book (New York: Solo Roma, 2015), p. 121.

4. NOVA, "Invisible Universe Revealed," written and directed by Peter Yost (PBS, April 22, 2015).

Notes to Principle 3

1. George Orwell, "In Front of Your Nose," http://orwell.ru/library/articles/nose/english/e_nose. Accessed March 2, 2017.

Notes to Chapter 10

1. Bourree Lam, "Learning to Listen, with the Help of Improv," The Atlantic, April 22, 2016, https://www.theatlantic.com/business/archive/2016/04/improv-teacher/479424/. Accessed September 26, 2017.

2. Sherry Turkle, Reclaiming Conversation: The Power of Talk in a Digital Age (New York: Penguin Books, 2015).

3. Timothy W. O'Brien, "The Art of Prayer," America Magazine, February 13, 2012, http://www.americamagazine.org/issue/5128/faith-focus/art-prayer. Accessed September 26, 2017.

4. NOVA, "Invisible Universe Revealed," written and directed by Peter Yost (PBS, April 22, 2015).

Notes to Chapter 11

1. Nicholas Carr, "Is Google Making Us Stupid?," *The Atlantic*, July/August 2008, https://www.theatlantic.com/magazine/archive/2008/07/is-google-making-us-stupid/306868/.

2. Daniel T. Willingham, "Smartphones Don't Make Us Dumb," *New York Times*, January 20, 2015, https://www.nytimes.com/2015/01/21/opinion/smartphones-dont-make-us-dumb.html?_r=0. Accessed September 26, 2017.

3. Brené Brown, "The Power of Vulnerability," June 2010. Video file retrieved from https://www.ted.com/talks/brene_brown_on_vulnerability. Accessed November 10, 2017.

4. Hayles, quoted by Jocelyn K. Glei, Deep Attention v. Hyper Attention, 99U, http://99u.com/workbook/13355/hyper-attention-vs-deep-attention. Accessed March 2, 2017.

5. T. J. Jagodowski, David Pasquesi, and Pam Victor, *Improvisation at the Speed of Life: The TJ and Dave Book* (New York: Solo Roma, 2015), p. 73.

6. Gene Weingarten, "Pearls before Breakfast: Can one of the nation's great musicians cut through the fog of a D.C. rush hour? Let's find out," *Washington Post Magazine*, April 8, 2007, https://www.washingtonpost.com/lifestyle/magazine/pearls-before-breakfast-can-one-of-the-nations-great-musicians-cut-through-the-fog-of-a-dc-rush-hour-lets-find-out/2014/09/23/8a6d46da-4331-11e4-b47c-f5889e061e5f_story.html?utm_term=.0d6f3b104a0c. Accessed September 26, 2017.

7. Chris Gethard, "A Lesson in Improv Technique," The Awesomer, http://theawesomer.com/a-lesson-on-improv-technique/364858/. Accessed March 2, 2017.

8. "The Everlasting Today of God," dotCommonweal, https://www.commonwealmagazine.org/blog/everlasting-today-god. Accessed March 2, 2017.

Notes to Chapter 12

1. David Hajdu, "Wynton's Blues," *The Atlantic*, March 2003, https://www.theatlantic.com/magazine/archive/2003/03/wyntons -blues/302684/. Accessed September 26, 2017.

2. Wendell Berry, "Manifesto: The Mad Farmer Liberation Front," in *The Country of Marriage* (San Diego: Harcourt Brace Jovanovich, 1973).

3. Sheryl Sandberg, "It's the hard days that determine who you are," *Boston Globe*, May 16, 2016, https://www.bostonglobe.com/opin ion/2016/05/16/hard-days-that-determine-who-you-are/3R5MODlB 8w8QcDt8X8BlEO/story.html. Accessed September 26, 2017.

Notes to Principle 4

1. Jodi Picoult, *Second Glance* (New York: Simon & Schuster, 2003), p. 450.

Notes to Chapter 13

1. Emma Allen, "How the Upright Citizens Brigade Improvised a Comedy Empire," *The New Yorker*, September 5, 2016, http://www .newyorker.com/magazine/2016/09/05/upright-citizens-brigades -comedy-empire. Accessed October 3, 2017.

2. "Wade Davis Explorers Bio," *National Geographic*, http://www .nationalgeographic.com/explorers/bios/wade-davis/. Accessed March 2, 2017.

3. James Surowiecki, *The Wisdom of Crowds* (New York: Random House, 2005), p. 4.

4. *Bull Durham*, directed by Ron Shelton (1998; 20th Century Fox), Blu-Ray.

Notes to Chapter 14

1. Carrie Stephanie, "Pirate, Robot or Ninja? UCB Vet Billy Merritt's Theory on the Three Types of Improv Performers," LA Weekly, January 16, 2012, http://www.laweekly.com/arts/pirate-robot-or-ninja-ucb-vet-billy-merritts-theory-on-the-three-types-of-improv-performers-2372357. Accessed October 3, 2017.

2. Lisa Kays, "Pirate, Ninjas and Robots: On stage and off?," The Improvisational Therapist, May 4, 2016, http://yesandtherapist.tumblr.com/post/143853515695/pirate-ninjas-and-robots-on-stage-and-off. Accessed October 3, 2017.

Notes to Chapter 15

1. Bill McKibben, quoted in Patricia Madson, Improv Wisdom: Don't Prepare, Just Show Up (New York: Bell Tower Books, 2005), p. 130.

2. Carrie Newcomer, "The Beautiful Not Yet," http://carrienewcomer.com/content/beautiful-not-yet. Accessed March 2, 2017.

3. Madson, Improv Wisdom, p. 88.

Notes to Chapter 16

1. Samuel Wells, "Improvising Leadership," Faith and Leadership, March 26, 2012, http://www.faithandleadership.com/multimedia/samuel-wells-improvising-leadership. Accessed October 3, 2017.

2. L. Gregory Jones, "Self-sabotage through bureaucratic thinking," Faith and Leadership, January 12, 2016, https://www.faithandleadership.com/l-gregory-jones-self-sabotage-through-bureaucratic-thinking. Accessed October 3, 2017.

3. Draeke Baer, "Always Wear the Same Suit: Obama's Presidential Productivity Secrets," Fast Company, February 12, 2014, https://www.fastcompany.com/3026265/work-smart/always-wear-the-same-suit-obamas-presidential-productivity-secrets. Accessed October 3, 2017.

4. Barry Schwartz, The Paradox of Choice: Why More Is Less (New York: Harper Perennial, 2005), pp. 77–78.

Notes to Chapter 17

1. Andy Weir, *The Martian* (New York: Random House, 2011), p. 8.

2. George Plimpton, ed., *Writers at Work 08: The Paris Review Interviews* (New York: Penguin Books, 1988).

3. *Friends*, "The One with Monica and Chandler's Wedding, Part Two," directed by Kevin S. Bright and written by Marta Kauffman and David Crane (NBC, May 17, 2001).

4. Kelly Leonard and Tom Yorton, *Yes, And: How Improvisation Reverses "No, But" Thinking and Improves Creativity and Collaboration—Lessons from The Second City* (New York: HarperBusiness, 2015), p. 42.

5. Courtney E. Martin, "Re-Humanizer at Your Service," *On Being*, April 10, 2015, https://onbeing.org/blog/re-humanizer-at-your-service /7469/. Accessed October 12, 2017.

6. Jean Vanier, *Community and Growth* (Mahwah, NJ: Paulist Press, 1989).

Notes to Chapter 18

1. "Quotes," Dwight D. Eisenhower Presidential Library and Museum, https://www.eisenhower.archives.gov/all_about_ike/quotes. html. Accessed March 2, 2017.

2. Samuel Wells, "Improvising Leadership," *Faith and Leadership*, March 26, 2012, http://www.faithandleadership.com/multimedia/ samuel-wells-improvising-leadership. Accessed October 3, 2017.

3. Oliver Burkeman's book is quoted by Maria Popova, "Stop Overplanning: The Psychology of Why Excessive Goal-Setting Limits Our Happiness and Success," *Brain Pickings*, February 5, 2014, http:// www.brainpickings.org/index.php/2014/02/05/oliver-burkeman-anti dote-plans-uncertainty/. Accessed October 3, 2017.

4. Dewitt Jones, "Everyday Creativity with Dewitt Jones," transcript, accessed March 2, 2017, http://www.irms.org/wp-content/ uploads/2015/04/Everyday-Creativity-Transcript.pdf.

Notes to Chapter 19

1. Leo Babauta, "Learn from the Greats: 7 Writing Habits of Amazing Writers," http://writetodone.com/learn-from-the-greats-7-writing-habits-of-amazing-writers/. Accessed October 3, 2017.

2. Phil Hansen, "Embrace the Shake," TED Talk, recorded February 2013, https://www.ted.com/talks/phil_hansen_embrace_the_shake. Accessed October 3, 2017.

3. *The West Wing*, "The Debate," Season 7, Episode 7, directed by Alex Graves and written by Lawrence O'Donnell Jr. (NBC, November 6, 2005).

4. Leonard Bernstein Quotes, Classic FM, http://www.classicfm.com/composers/bernstein-l/guides/leonard-bernstein-quotes/music/. Accessed March 2, 2017.

Notes to Principle 6

1. Samuel Wells, *Improvisation: The Drama of Christian Ethics* (Grand Rapids: Brazos Press, 2004), p. 45.

Notes to Chapter 20

1. Christopher Ingraham, "America's top fears: Public speaking, heights and bugs," *Washington Post*, October 30, 2014, https://www.washingtonpost.com/news/wonk/wp/2014/10/30/clowns-are-twice-as-scary-to-democrats-as-they-are-to-republicans/?utm_term=.4ff90aef4f91. Accessed October 4, 2017.

2. Maria Popova, "The Taste Gap: Ira Glass on the Secret of Creative Success, Animated in Living Typography," *Brain Pickings*, January 29, 2014, https://www.brainpickings.org/2014/01/29/ira-glass-success-daniel-sax/. Accessed October 4, 2017.

3. T. J. Jagodowski, David Pasquesi, and Pam Victor, *Improvisation at the Speed of Life: The TJ and Dave Book* (New York: Solo Roma, 2015), p. 119.

4. "Strategy: William Stafford—'Lower your standards,'" *Rooze*, http://www.beltwaypoetry.com/william-stafford/. Accessed October 4, 2017.

5. Patricia Madson, *Improv Wisdom: Don't Prepare, Just Show Up* (New York: Bell Tower Books, 2005), p. 62.

Notes to Chapter 21

1. Johnstone, quoted by Samuel Wells, *Improvisation: The Drama of Christian Ethics* (Grand Rapids: Brazos Press, 2004), p. 126.

2. Samuel Wells, "Improvising Leadership," *Faith and Leadership*, March 26, 2012, http://www.faithandleadership.com/multimedia/samuel-wells-improvising-leadership. Accessed October 4, 2017.

3. Annie Dillard, *The Writing Life* (New York: Harper Perennial, 2013), p. 78.

4. T. J. Jagodowski, David Pasquesi, and Pam Victor, *Improvisation at the Speed of Life: The TJ and Dave Book* (New York: Solo Roma, 2015), p. 22.

5. Walter Brueggemann, "The Liturgy of Abundance, The Myth of Scarcity," *Christian Century*, March 24, 1999, http://wearethewalking dead.weebly.com/survival-tools/the-liturgy-of-abundance-the-myth -of-scarcity-by-walter-brueggemann. Accessed October 4, 2017.

6. Twist, quoted by Brene Brown, "Enough," May 5, 2008, http://brenebrown.com/2008/05/05/200855enough-html/. Accessed October 4, 2017.

Notes to Chapter 22

1. "Herbie Hancock on Miles Davis," YouTube video, posted by Old Town Improv Co., April 13, 2016, https://www.youtube.com/watch?v=t-vItf0G05M. Accessed October 4, 2017.

2. Jake Falce, "Life as Jazz: When You Hit a 'Wrong' Note, Improvise," *Hartford Courant*, March 30, 2016, http://www.courant.com/opin ion/op-ed/hc-op-fresh-talk-falce-dont-fear-mistakes-0330–20160329 -story.html.

3. Patrick Gantz, "Patterns and Games Montage," https://improv doesbest.com/2015/12/22/patterns-and-games-montage/. Accessed March 2, 2017.

4. Sally Schneider, "Falling (and Failing) as Essential Practice and

Play," *Improvised Life*, February 25, 2016, http://www.improvisedlife
.com/2016/02/25/falling-practice-play/.

5. Aza Raskin, "You Are Solving the Wrong Problem," http://www
.azarask.in/blog/post/the-wrong-problem/. Accessed March 2, 2017.

6. Richard Rohr, *Falling Upward: A Spirituality for the Two Halves of
Life* (San Francisco: Jossey-Bass, 2011), p. 128.

7. "The Powerful Lesson Maya Angelou Taught Oprah," Oprah
.com, http://www.oprah.com/oprahs-lifeclass/the-powerful-lesson
-maya-angelou-taught-oprah-video. Accessed March 2, 2017.

Notes to Chapter 23

1. I credit Eugenia Gamble with these words, though she makes it
clear they are not original to her. They are believed to be a Franciscan
blessing, but scholars have been unable to trace the origin.

2. Maria Popova, "Why the Best Roadmap to an Interesting
Life Is the One You Make Up as You Go Along: Daniel Pink's Commencement Address," *Brain Pickings*, http://www.brainpickings.org/
index.php/2014/06/25/daniel-pink-northwestern-commencement/.
Accessed October 4, 2017.

3. Joan Chittister, *Between the Dark and the Daylight: Embracing the
Contradictions of Life* (New York: Crown Publishing Group, 2015), p. 40.

Notes to Principle 7

1. Isak Dinesen, "The Monkey," in *Seven Gothic Tales* (New York:
Vintage Books, 1991).

Notes to Chapter 24

1. David Bentley Hart, *The Doors of the Sea: Where Was God in the
Tsunami?* (Grand Rapids: Eerdmans, 2005), p. 99.

2. *Frontline*, "Faith and Doubt at Ground Zero," written and directed by Helen Whitney (PBS, September 3, 2002); Brad Hirschfield
is quoted.

Notes to Chapter 25

1. David Brooks, "The Summoned Self," *New York Times*, August 2, 2010, http://www.nytimes.com/2010/08/03/opinion/03brooks.html. Accessed October 4, 2017.

2. Frederick Buechner, *Wishful Thinking: A Seeker's ABC* (San Francisco: HarperOne, 1993), pp. 118–19.

3. Howard Thurman, quoted by Gill Baille, *Violence Unveiled: Humanity at the Crossroads* (New York: Crossroad Publishing Company, 1996), p. xv.

4. Mike Rowe, "It's a Dirty Job, and I Love It!" *Forbes*, December 9, 2008, https://www.forbes.com/2008/12/09/mike-rowe-jobs-lead -careers-employment08-cx_mr_1209rowe.html. Accessed October 4, 2017.

5. Rick Steves, quoted by Patricia Madson, *Improv Wisdom: Don't Prepare, Just Show Up* (New York: Bell Tower Books, 2005), p. 141.

Notes to Chapter 26

1. Rami Shapiro, *Wisdom of the Jewish Sages: A Modern Reading of Pirke Avot* (New York: Harmony/Bell Tower Books, 1995), p. 41.

2. *The Lord of the Rings: The Two Towers*, directed by Peter Jackson (2002; New Line Home Entertainment, 2003), DVD.

3. *The Hunger Games*, directed by Gary Ross (2012, Color Force; Lionsgate, 2012), DVD.

4. Sally Schneider, "Batali's Beautiful 'F--- You': A Tale of 9/11," *Improvised Life*, September 11, 2011, http://www.improvisedlife .com/2011/09/11/batalis-beautiful-fuck-you-a-tale-of-911/. Accessed October 4, 2017.

5. Craig Barnes, "Boxed In," *Christian Century*, August 15, 2013, https://www.christiancentury.org/article/2013–08/boxed. Accessed October 4, 2017.

Acknowledgments

For all that has been—Thanks!
For all that will be—Yes.

—Dag Hammarskjöld

To my fellow improvisers: Marthame Sanders, Allison Gilmore, and Jim Karwisch; Ashley Goff and Casey FitzGerald; the Theology of Improv Facebook group; Jarad Schofer and Sexy Lawn Guy; Coonoor Behal, Erick Acuña, and Crazy Eights; JC Calcerano and everyone at WIT; Liz Joynt Sandberg, Jeannie Cahill Griggs, Jay Steigmann, Jimmy Carrane, and everyone with whom I played in Chicago; Bagelz and Jam; Lisa Kays and the clergy improvisers; and LeAnn Hodges, David Westerlund, Paul Vasile, and Marthame for making magic happen in Kansas City.

I am thankful to the Louisville Institute for the Pastoral Study Grant that helped this book move from a hodgepodge of ideas to an organized piece of work, and to the Collegeville Institute for serving as an incubator at an opportune time. Lil Copan, Mary Hietbrink, Rachel Brewer, and the entire Eerdmans team gave this book their most enthusiastic support, and for that I am grateful.

Countless congregations (as well as Columbia Theological Seminary) invited me to come and share this content through retreats, conferences, sermons, and classes. Thank you for your openness, your questions, and your sense of adventure, all of which helped shape this book. Andrew Foster Connors, Lisa Hamilton, Mara Rosenberg, Keith Snyder, and Beth Palmer offered their experience and heart—thank you.

I couldn't have done this without my family, especially my mother, in-laws, and siblings, and my chosen families: the Well, RtR, MRTT, Gini/Kelly/Kristen, the Ragnarians, and the Badass Clergywomen.

And Robert. Our family is my greatest Yes. Thank you doesn't feel like enough, but it's all I have to offer, which means it is enough indeed.